Puddings

Puddings

Johnny Shepherd

Over 100 classic puddings from cakes, tarts, crumbles and pies to all things chocolatey

*This book is for every
St Albans commuter
who has ever stopped
by the Pudmobile.
Without you The
Pudding Stop would
not be where it is
today, and that means
more than I could
ever explain.*

Contents

Introduction

Puddings Through Time

There is no doubt that English pudding is a tradition that is centuries old – and with a well-deserved reputation. Pudding came from the French word *boudin*, or sausage. The oldest type of pudding was boiled in animal intestine – among its surviving relatives are black pudding and haggis, favourites of Henry VIII. The intestine, typically from a sheep or pig, formed a useful natural casing to be filled with ingredients. In fact, the original Christmas pudding contained minced beef, dried fruit, sugar and oats held together and boiled within an intestine, finished off by toasting or baking over embers.

However, filling an animal skin required thorough cleaning and was a tricky process. Boiling the pudding mixture in a cloth became a more practical alternative. In the seventeenth century, the pudding cloth featured in every British kitchen and cooks became more creative in the types of pudding they made. Best known are suet-based puddings, such as plum pudding and steak and kidney pudding, but there were many others. Sir Kenelm Digby's Quaking Pudding – custard cooked in a cloth-lined basin without suet – was light and wobbly.

Over time, sweet and savoury ingredients were separated from the same pudding, although once wrapped in cloth they often shared the same boiling pot or plate. Plum pudding was served alongside roast beef long before the battered Yorkshire pudding took over. Bone marrow was used to enrich the puddings, and sweet puddings were beginning to emerge, making good use of sugar being imported from the Caribbean. By the late seventeenth century, puddings were championed by King George I – known as The Pudding King – and sweet steamed and baked puddings became popular. Cooks incorporated dried fruits, candied peel, spices, fresh fruit and nuts. Eating sweet puddings became a sign of wealth as more and more exotic and scarce ingredients were sourced.

By the time of the Industrial Revolution, homes had ovens in their chimney breasts, providing a simple way to bake puddings. At this point puddings were either boiled or baked in pudding basins rather than cloth. The Industrial Revolution created jobs for the working classes; their husbands' salary enabled housewives to purchase ingredients; better transport networks lowered food prices and different fruits could be picked and incorporated into puddings as they emerged throughout the seasons.

By the end of the nineteenth century, puddings were a staple in every British home, with housewives and housemaids seeking new ideas and inspiration from cookbooks such as Eliza Acton's *Modern Cookbook for Private Families* in 1845 or Mrs Beeton's *Book of Household Management* in 1861. Puddings continued to evolve over the next century as new ingredients were sourced and recipes shared. Different puddings became associated with specific regions of Britain and often took the name of towns or counties. Eponymous puddings include Bakewell tart, Eccles cake, Huntingdon pudding, Cambridge burnt cream and Norfolk tart, a couple of which I've included in this book.

Two world wars forced families to live off rations, and cooks had to cut back and come up with alternative puddings. Most famously crumble developed from housewives not having sufficient butter in their weekly ration pack to make pastry. Furthermore, like many great inventions, new puddings emerged serendipitously. This was particularly true when the Tatin sisters incorrectly cooked an apple pie one night at their family-owned hotel in France. Luckily, their customers loved it and so the new pudding remained – tarte tatin.

Over the last 50 years, cooking and baking has become accessible to all, and recipe inspiration taken from television, cookbooks and magazines. Particular puddings have become family favourites – associated with happy times and fond memories, and their recipes updated and treasured for future generations.

Today though, living in an increasingly health-conscious society, pudding (and the interchangeable dessert) has become a dirty word – deemed unnecessary by some in a world where levels of childhood and adult obesity has soared. The commercialisation of puddings – with the inclusion of chemical flavours and colours, oil and egg substitutes, premixed packets, milk powder, chemical preservatives and stabilisers – has not helped. Sadly, puddings were among the first victims of mass catering and manufacturing. Visit any well-known high street restaurant today and the chances are the puddings – created with shelf life and bottom line in mind – will have been made well in advance with added chemicals that, if you were to make them yourself at home, you would certainly not add.

Homemade puddings do contain calorific ingredients – such as sugar, dried fruits and nuts, chocolate, butter, cream and milk – but as part of a healthy and balanced diet, they contribute great pleasure. There's a lot to be said for the health and happiness of a person with an appetite and a love of proper food. English puddings have a renowned reputation and quite rightly so. In her book *English Food*, Jane Grigson describes English puddings as 'wonderful things . . . of the most subtle and imaginative combinations, relying on simple and natural ingredients'. And like Jane, I think there is a lot to be said for a nation that has brought people up on apple crumble and custard!

The Pudding Stop

Growing up in a family of bakers, food was central to all gatherings. I've known and enjoyed good pudding from a young age. In particular I remember my mother's treacle sponge and custard on a cold school night or Grandma's jam roly poly steamed in her fish kettle. Pudding is associated with strong family memories and happy times, with the family together around a big table chatting for hours, eating seconds and sometimes eating thirds.

In my twenties living away from home, I realised it was difficult to find good pudding; unless I was at a restaurant with an in-house pastry chef (a rarity on the high street), no one else's puds would do. This got me thinking – are many people disappointed with pudding options? Could a place that just serves pudding be popular?

I tested this very simply at my local market to see if the puddings I made were popular and if customers would come back again and again. They did. Over time I discovered that markets were fickle places. The perishable nature of freshly made pud demanded a more permanent pitch. Thereafter, the Pudmobile was born. At my local train station, with plenty of commuters from London as customers and a stack of puddings to sell, I quickly built up a loyal fan base. Stopping by the Pudmobile rewarded a long day in the City or said sorry for getting home late.

The next step was a place where I could bake and sell all in one place. A shop.
The Pudding Stop.

This book includes the recipes that I grew up on and puds served regularly at The Pudding Stop. There's a familiarity to the puddings because I look to my family and the seasons to inspire them. There's no fuss, no fads, just tasty puddings, which are baked and prepared fresh each day in our bakery and served in the shop or from the Pudmobile every weeknight.

Use this book to create these puddings at home. Every time you open it, pick puddings for the season (when a fruit is at its natural best), choose puddings for the people you love and happy memories will be made.

Ingredients

The ingredients for these recipes are humble and relatively cheap to buy. I urge you to buy the best quality you can; it really will make a difference to the final puddings. Take for instance my recipe for sticky toffee pudding, in which I suggest the inclusion of a double shot of tasty espresso from a local independent coffee shop – to add espresso that is not tasty is pointless. Or for my custard tart, where organic free-range eggs are essential to achieve rich yellow custard. My approach to puddings is simple, but simplicity demands the best ingredients.

Top Tips for Best Baking

- Always use unsalted, and organic British butter if possible.

- Buy chocolate from good-quality online suppliers (www.beantobarchocolate.co.uk) for best results. The majority of my recipes use dark chocolate with a minimum of 70 per cent cocoa solids.

- Always use 100 per cent cocoa powder for the proper chocolate flavour in the puddings. The recipes contain sufficient sugar to ensure there won't be any bitterness.

- All my recipes use full-fat milk and double cream; look out for both at your local farmers' market – there are fewer dairy farmers out there these days. Yeo Valley does a good range of organic milk, cream and butter if you are buying from the supermarket.

- The majority of my fruit-based recipes include British fruits, so try and catch them at the right time of the year.

- All of our flour is organic from Shipton Mill in the Cotswolds, they stock and mill every type of flour you could possibly need.

- Honey, maple syrup, black treacle and golden syrup feature in many of my puddings. If you can get yourself down to your local cash and carry to buy these things in bulk they will be significantly cheaper and have a brilliant shelf life. For maple syrup visit health food stores to get pure maple syrup, and try to source local honey at a farmers' market.

- All of the recipes that include sea salt flakes use Maldon.

- Use unrefined raw cane sugar if you can. Soft light brown and dark brown sugar are good to use in baking as they add wonderful caramel notes to a pudding.

- Often in the book I suggest the addition of a bottle of something fine, such as Poire William or Pedro Ximenez sherry – although the recipes won't be quite the same if you leave them out, they are optional. I suggest you purchase them with the view to drinking the remainder of the bottle, as otherwise you will find yourself with several unfinished bottles.

How to Steam a Pudding

I am a huge fan of steaming as a method of cooking puddings and lots of the recipes in the book are cooked in this way. It is incredibly simple to do using equipment I'm sure you have at home.

What you need: baking parchment • scissors • pudding basin • foil string • saucepan & lid

To make the circle (cartouche), take a piece of baking parchment and fold it in half and then half again. Fold one side into the middle centre line as if you were making a paper aeroplane.

Using the pointy end, measure from the middle of you pudding basin to the outer rim and then a further 2 inches outwards. Using scissors, cut a curve at the end of the parchment. Unfold your cartouche so that it fits comfortably over the pudding basin.

Take a piece of foil to cover the parchment and fold a pleat in the middle. Lay the parchment, followed by the foil, over the top of the pudding basin and tie tightly with string to form a water-tight seal.

The pudding is now ready to be placed inside a pan. Ensure the base of the pudding bowl is not in direct contact with the base of the pan. Add enough water to reach halfway up the sides of the pudding bowl and cover the pan tightly with the lid. Steam the pudding according to my specific recipe instructions.

Equipment

The beauty of baking is that anyone can do it and you don't need fancy equipment. All that's really needed is a big bowl, a spoon and plenty of enthusiasm and elbow grease. However, every year you grow older and as a reward friends and family could buy you some of the following:

Useful Kit

- The first gift should be a really decent pair of digital scales that you can plug in to charge – they will cost, but they are essential to consistent results with your baking.

- Choose the biggest stainless steel mixing bowl you can fit in your cupboard and a few little ones. They're very useful when cracking and separating eggs.

- Electricity has made us lazy: a bad combination when mixed with puddings. But a KitchenAid stand mixer makes everything easier. When things are easy you're calm and the ingredients will sense your calmness; they will behave and you'll have really good results.

- I find a spatula one of the most useful pieces of kit in my kitchen. You can clean them easily and they allow you to get every last morsel of mixture from a mixing bowl. Which is ESSENTIAL when you run a food business or have a big appetite.

- Sometimes you don't have enough mixture to warrant using an electric mixer, or a concoction has split beyond recognition. This is when a flexible stainless steel balloon whisk will solve all your problems and save a batch of batter from the bin.

Get hold of the following tins and pudding basins and you'll be able to make and bake everything in my book:

- *small dariole moulds or ramekin dishes*
- *23cm and 30cm fluted tart tins*
- *23cm round loose-bottomed cake tin*
- *8 or 12-hole muffin and mince pie tins*
- *900g loaf tin*
- *30 x 40cm Swiss roll tin*
- *25 x 35 x 5cm deep-sided roasting tin*
- *23 x 23 x 5cm square baking tin*
- *28 x 5cm round ceramic pie dish*
- *500ml and 1-litre ceramic ovenproof pudding basins*

And finally, once you have all this cool kit in your cupboard, you can get stuck into this book! Good luck and may all creations be fuelled by enthusiasm to feed friends and family for many years to come.

Crumbly & Crunchy

Pastry: Shortcrust, Sweet, Almond,
Polenta, Quick Puff & Suet

Treacle Tart

Bakewell Tart or Pudding

Pecan Pie

Pear Strudel

Quince Cobbler

Lemon & Polenta Cake

Kenny's Crumble Cake

Plum Crumble

Poor Knights of Windsor

Queen of Puddings

The Romans were the first to develop pastry from a rough mix of flour and water – a paste primarily used to protect meat and game juices during roasting. Pastry was never actually eaten until it became enriched with eggs and fat such as suet, lard or butter. Through medieval times and into the seventeenth century, pastry making became well established, creating new and varied forms including what we know today as suet, shortcrust, sweet, puff and many other types of pastry.

If you can master pastry, then you will never need to buy a pudding again, nor will you have any disappointed diners. Pastry contains humble ingredients, with just skill and time being the barrier to consistent results. However, use my recipes, practise regularly and you will have a new skill for life – and homemade pastry proudly placed in your armoury. Once mastered, a wondrous array of puddings opens up to you, from English classics like Bakewell and treacle tart to European imports such as strudel and pastel de nata.

Pastry can be crumbly or crunchy, often depending on whether it lies above or beneath the heartbeat of a pudding. A crumble topping is essentially a pastry with the absence of egg or water to bind it. It achieves both crumbly and crunchy textures once baked and is perhaps the finest and simplest of English puddings. Even so, many more puddings offer these wonderful textures, such as those made with my melt-in-the-mouth crumbly shortcrust pastry or my version of a lemon and polenta cake with course polenta and added crunch from a demerara sugar drizzle.

Puddings can have textural pleasures beyond one dimension, and it is often those that combine a silky smooth filling with a crunchy or crumbly topping that please the most.

Pastry

Pastry is an incredibly useful thing to have in the fridge, and having it ready to go for next time will encourage you to bake at home more often.

Shortcrust Pastry

This is your everyday melt-in-the-mouth pastry. It will form the shell for tarts, such as spiced nectarine tart, mincemeat tart and my baked chocolate tart. Use this pastry when you have a very sweet filling, to balance out the sweetness.

Makes 425g pastry

225g plain flour, siefted

120g cold unsalted butter (or you a mix of 60g butter and 60g cold lard)

50g icing sugar

A pinch of sea salt flakes

2 tablespoons cold water

Put the flour in a large bowl. Cut the butter and lard into little cubes and rub into the flour with your fingertips. Stop when most of the fat has been incorporated but you can still see some of it in clumps.

Stir in the icing sugar and salt.

Make a well in the centre of the mixture and pour in the cold water. Bring the pastry together into a dough using your hands. Tip the dough out onto a lightly floured surface and knead a couple of times to get it into a nice ball before wrapping in cling film ready to be chilled. Chill for at least 30 minutes before baking as instructed. The dough can be kept for a couple of days as it is in the fridge, or frozen for a month. Allow the dough to come to a pliable texture before rolling when it has been chilled for a long time.

Tip: This makes enough to line one 23cm tart tin.

Sweet Pastry

This pastry is really easy to work with and foolproof – no matter how bad your pastry skills are, following these simple steps will give you perfect results every time. This pastry will form the shell for delicious fillings, such as pecan pie, custard tart and more throughout this book.

Makes 450g pastry

125g unsalted butter

60g caster sugar

1 egg, beaten

250g plain flour, siefted, plus extra for dusting

½ teaspoon sea salt flakes

Cream the butter and sugar together in a stand mixer until pale and fluffy. Slowly add the beaten egg and mix well.

Stop the mixer and add the flour and salt. Carefully turn the mixer back on at the slowest speed and let the flour mix into the creamed butter for half a dozen turns, or until the mixture resembles pastry.

Turn the dough out onto a lightly floured work surface and knead with your hands to form a nice ball of pastry before wrapping in cling film ready for the fridge. Chill for at least 30 minutes before baking as instructed. The dough can be kept for a couple of days as it is in the fridge, or frozen for a month. Allow the dough to come to a pliable texture before rolling when it has been chilled for a long time.

Tip: If your dough is too wet when you are kneading, add a small handful of flour to bring it together – the pastry must be dry and almost ready to roll before it's chilled.

This makes enough to line one 23cm tart tin.

Almond Pastry

This pastry recreates the melt-in-the-mouth texture of shortcrust with the ease of working with sweet pastry. This works really well with any of the recipes, but perhaps save it for special occasions, as the almonds create a richer and more decadent pastry.

Makes 325g pastry

120g unsalted butter

50g caster sugar

1 egg, beaten

165g plain flour, sifted, plus extra for dusting

25g ground almonds

A pinch of sea salt flakes

Cream the butter and sugar together in a stand mixer until pale and fluffy. Slowly add the beaten egg and mix well.

Stop the mixer and add all the flour, ground almonds and salt. Carefully turn the mixer back on at the slowest speed and let the flour mix into the creamed butter for half a dozen turns, or until the mixture resembles pastry.

Turn the dough out onto a lightly floured work surface and knead with your hands to form a nice ball of pastry, before wrapping in cling film ready for the fridge. Chill for at least 30 minutes before baking as instructed. The dough can be kept for a couple of days as it is in the fridge, or frozen for a month. Allow the dough to come to a pliable texture before rolling when it has been chilled for a long time.

Tip: This makes enough to line one 23cm tart tin.

Polenta Pastry

Many of my recipes would be gluten-free, were it not for flour-fuelled pastry – things like Bakewell tart or pecan pie, for example. This pastry must be well chilled and you may have to patch up a few holes when lining the tin – but it works, and once you've nailed it you can bake gluten-free Bakewell after gluten-free Bakewell.

Makes 485g pastry

100g unsalted butter

85g sugar

1 egg

A pinch of sea salt

150g ground almonds

150g fine polenta

Cream the butter and sugar together in a bowl until pale and fluffy. Add the egg and the salt, followed by the almonds and polenta. Bring all the ingredients together and knead lightly. Once the dough is formed and smooth, wrap in cling film and chill for 1 hour before using.

Tip: This makes enough to line one 23cm tart tin.

Quick Puff Pastry

Few people make their own puff pastry as it's much easier to buy the ready-made variety. However, it's not difficult to make – it just takes time and patience to create the layers. My super-speedy version eliminates much of this painstaking effort and yields excellent results. It is by no means instant, but who wants instant anyway – good things come to those who wait!

Makes 350g pastry

125g strong white bread flour, sifted, plus extra for dusting

25g icing sugar

125g unsalted French butter, cut into cubes

1 teaspoon lemon juice

A pinch sea salt flakes

50ml ice-cold water

Weigh the flour and icing sugar into a bowl, and rub in 25g of the butter with your fingers. Add the remaining butter and toss with your fingertips to ensure each piece of butter is covered.

Mix the lemon juice and salt with the water and pour it into the flour and butter, wetting as much flour as possible and press all together into rough dough.

Turn it out onto a floured work surface and shape into a small rectangle. Roll out into a rectangle about 1cm thick, flouring all the time to prevent the pastry from sticking.

Take both of the short ends (top and bottom) and fold them over to meet in the middle. Fold over again along the central divide to make a book shape. Turn the spine of the pastry book to your right, roll out again and fold as before – again flouring as you go.

If the pastry is too soft at this point you won't be able to use it yet – place it in the fridge or freezer to chill until hard and continue.

Once finished, you can use it to line a muffin tin for Portuguese custard tarts, a tart tin for a Bakewell pudding or free-formed to make a strudel. Remember to chill the unfilled, lined pastry tin for 30 minutes before the pastry is baked with whatever filling you choose.

Suet Pastry

Suet has been added to puddings since they were first served at tables centuries ago. It is a wonderful naturally occurring product that has similar properties to butter. But unlike butter, it forms a soft pliable pastry as opposed to a crisp crumbly pastry. This means that it provides an incredible base for many puddings; it forms a texture in between a pastry and a sponge, meaning it will soak up any juices nearby. My recipe creates a really light suet pastry, which works just as well lining a pudding basin for my pond pudding, as making a spotted dick or a free-formed roly poly pudding . . . warm jam roly poly and custard on a cold winter's night, yum!

Makes 550g pastry

250g self-raising flour, sifted

A pinch of fine sea salt

1 teaspoon baking powder

100g suet

100ml buttermilk

100ml water

zest of one orange (optional)

Mix the flour, salt, baking powder and suet in a bowl.

Mix the buttermilk and water together in a bowl, then slowly pour this into the dry ingredients. Mix together with your hands or a spoon until the mixture has formed a soft dough that is easy to handle. You may not need all of the wet ingredients. It can be used straight away or chilled for later.

Tip: Add the zest of one orange when mixing the ingredients for a frangrant dough.

Treacle Tart

In 1883 Lyle, the manufacturer of black treacle, created a sweeter liquid sugar – golden syrup. Henceforth, all sugar syrup was known as treacle. Thrifty home cooks mixed it with breadcrumbs and it nourished the whole family. My treacle tart counters this sweet syrup with orange and eggs to create an unctuous middle and a crunchy top.

Serves 12

1 batch of Shortcrust Pastry (see page 20)

Flour, for dusting

700g golden syrup

Grated zest and juice of 1 orange

175g crumbed brioche (for richness) or sourdough (for flavour)

3 large eggs, lightly whisked

A pinch of sea salt

Roll out the pastry on a lightly floured work surface to about 3mm thick. Use it to line a greased 23cm loose-bottomed tart tin, prick all over with a fork and chill for 30 minutes. Preheat the oven to 180°C/160°C fan/350°F/Gas mark 4.

Line the pastry shell with foil, pushing it in at the edges, and fill to the top with baking beans. Bake for about 15 minutes, or until lightly golden. Remove the foil and baking beans and return the pastry case to the oven for 1 minute. Remove from the oven (leaving the oven on) and leave to cool.

Meanwhile, make the filling. Pour the golden syrup into a pan, add the orange zest and juice and set over a medium heat until warm. Stir in the breadcrumbs, remove from the heat and leave for 10 minutes, or until the golden syrup has been absorbed by the breadcrumbs. Add the eggs and salt and stir through.

Pour the treacle filling into the tart case and bake for 35–40 minutes, until firm to the touch and golden brown. Serve warm with clotted cream, vanilla ice cream or both.

Tip: Leaving the tart to cool for 10 minutes before cutting with a sharp bread knife (and a sense of purpose!) is a good idea.

Variation: For a twist on this recipe try folding 175g shelled walnuts into the mixture before pouring into the tart shell.

Bakewell Tart or Pudding

From the eponymous market town in Derbyshire comes a pudding that brings much joy to the English. That combination of warm jam, soft frangipane and crunchy toasted almonds, all served with cold ice cream or thick custard is timeless. Bakewell tart uses shortcrust pastry while the original Bakewell pudding calls for puff – both work magically.

Serves 8–10

1 batch of Shortcrust Pastry (see page 20) or 1 batch of Quick Puff Pastry (see page 23)

Flour, for dusting

385g jam (raspberry jam is traditional – see Tip below)

65g unsalted butter

A pinch of salt

165g caster sugar

4 large eggs

165g ground almonds

1 teaspoon almond extract

A liberal handful of flaked almonds to cover

Roll out the pastry on a lightly floured work surface to about 3mm thick. Use it to line a greased 23cm loose-bottomed tart tin, prick all over with a fork and chill for 30 minutes.

Spoon the jam into a bowl and stir to loosen it if necessary. Spread the jam evenly over the pastry and return it to the fridge while you make the filling.

Preheat the oven to 180°C/160°C fan/350°F/Gas mark 4.

Cream the butter, salt and sugar together in a bowl until pale and fluffy. Lightly beat the eggs, then add them to the butter mixture a little at a time with a handful of ground almonds when necessary to prevent the mixture from curdling. Once all the egg has been combined stir in the remaining ground almonds and the almond extract.

Pour the filling into the tart case and liberally sprinkle over the flaked almonds. Bake for 35–40 minutes, until firm to the touch and golden brown.

Leave to cool, then slice with a bread knife for a clean cut – sawing like a piece of wood rather than pushing downward. To serve warm, place slices on individual plates and into an oven preheated to 150°C/130°C fan/300°F/Gas mark 2 for 5–10 minutes. Serve with vanilla ice cream, custard or both.

Tip: At the shop, we change the jam used according to the season – apricot, plum, damson and gooseberry all make a very fine Bakewell.

Pecan Pie

Pecan pie is a staple of the southern states of North America and is synonymous with Thanksgiving. Corn syrup with pecans is the most traditional combination, but it is perfectly fine to use a combination of maple or golden syrup and brown sugar – you can even use walnuts if you're lucky enough to have a wild walnut tree growing near your house.

Serves 8–10

1 batch of Sweet Pastry (see page 21)

Flour, for dusting

150g unsalted butter

325 dark brown muscovado sugar

1 vanilla pod, split with seeds scraped out, or 1 teaspoon vanilla extract

A large pinch of sea salt

150g golden or maple syrup

4 large eggs

285g pecans, lightly crushed

Roll out the pastry on a lightly floured work surface to about 3mm thick. Use it to line a greased 23cm loose-bottomed tart tin, prick all over with a fork and chill for 30 minutes. Preheat the oven to 180°C/160°C fan/350°F/Gas mark 4.

Line the pastry shell with foil, pushing it in at the edges, and fill with baking beans. Bake for about 15 minutes, or until lightly golden. Remove the foil and baking beans and return the pastry case to the oven for about 1–2 minutes, until it is a good golden brown colour all over. Remove from the oven (leaving the oven on) and leave to cool.

Meanwhile, make the filling. Place the butter, sugar, vanilla, salt and golden syrup into a heavy pan and warm over a medium heat until completely melted. Remove from the heat, then whisk in the eggs when cool.

Put the shelled pecan halves into the baked pastry case and distribute evenly. Pour the filling over the pecans, re-distributing any pecans that have moved.

Bake for 30–40 minutes, or until the centre of the pie springs back when pressed. Remove from the oven and leave to cool slightly for 10 minutes or so before slicing and serving warm with vanilla ice cream.

Pear Strudel

For this traditional Austrian treat I like to use puff pastry rather than the more typical filo, as it transforms the strudel into a hearty pudding.

Serves 8–10

50g unsalted butter

8 large dessert pears, peeled, cored and diced

300g caster sugar

2 star anise

200g sultanas

2 batches of Quick Puff Pastry (see page 23)

1 large egg, beaten

Icing sugar, for sprinkling

Preheat the oven to 180°C/160°C fan/350°F/Gas mark 4 and line a baking tray with greaseproof paper.

Place a saucepan over a medium heat and melt the butter. Add the pears, caster sugar and star anise. Cook slowly for about 10–15 minutes, until the pears are soft and tender. Remove from the heat and strain the pears, reserving the cooking liquid in a saucepan.

Place the pan with the liquid in back over the heat and reduce to a sticky syrup. Remove from the heat and add the cooked pears and sultanas. Leave to cool in the fridge.

Roll out the puff pastry on a floured work surface into a 30 x 40cm rectangle, no more than 1cm thick. Carefully transfer the pastry to the prepared baking tray. Spread the cooled pear mixture over the pastry to cover the rectangle, leaving a 2.5cm border clear around the edge. Fold the short ends in by about 1cm. Brush the perimeter with beaten egg and fold the long edge closest to you over to seal the pears. Press down lightly or crimp to seal.

Use a sharp knife to make about five small slits along the top of the strudel to allow air to be released. Brush with the remaining beaten egg and sprinkle liberally with icing sugar. Bake for 35–40 minutes, or until golden brown. It is enjoyable warm or cold, but either way it is advisable to leave it to settle a little out of the oven before slicing. Dust with more icing sugar.

Quince Cobbler

The origin of the cobbler is said to be with British settlers in early British American colonies not having their typical pudding ingredients (suet) or equipment (pudding cloth) – instead they covered stewed fruit with a simple topping. The quince was the sacred fruit of Aphrodite – and I love quince in a cobbler. Make the dough the day before to ensure it's firm enough.

Serves 8

100g cold unsalted butter, diced

225g self-raising flour, sifted, plus extra for dusting

75g light brown soft sugar

A pinch of sea salt

1 teaspoon mixed spice

1 large egg, beaten, plus 1 more for glazing

75ml buttermilk (you may not need it all)

For the fruit

A small knob of butter

2 large Bramley apples (or any other good cooking apples), cored and cut into small cubes

5 large quinces, peeled, cored and sliced

3 handfuls of caster sugar, plus extra for sprinkling

100ml water

Rub the butter and flour together in a large bowl until you achieve fine breadcrumbs. Add the sugar, salt and mixed spice and mix through, then stir in the egg.

Make a well in the middle of the bowl and slowly pour in the buttermilk and gently mix until you have a soft but not too sticky dough.

Knead into a ball on a lightly floured work surface and wrap in cling film. Leave to rest in the fridge for at least 12 hours.

The filling can be made in advance as well. Add the knob of butter to a saucepan set over a medium heat. Add the apple, quince, caster sugar and water. Cook over a very low heat for about 45 minutes, or until the fruit is soft and tender. Remove from the heat and set aside if not cooking immediately, otherwise pour into a round 28 x 5cm ceramic crumble dish. Preheat the oven to 180°C/160°C fan/350°F/Gas mark 4.

On a lightly dusted work surface, roll out the cobbler dough to at least 1cm thick and cut into rounds using a pastry cutter – it doesn't really matter what size cutter you use, but I would avoid anything larger than 4cm.

Cover the fruit with the pastry rounds and brush with beaten egg to glaze. Sprinkle with a little extra caster sugar and bake for 30–40 minutes, or until the cobbler is golden brown and the juices of the apple and quince are seeping through. Eat straight away with cream or custard.

Lemon & Polenta Squares

This recipe is a homage to the classic cake made famous by The River Café and completely denounces any theory that gluten-free is a compromise. It has a great shelf life and is perfect with a cup of tea or warmed with extra lemon syrup as a pudding. Try to find Amalfi lemons if you can.

Makes 10 square slices

200g unsalted butter

275g caster sugar

1 teaspoon vanilla extract (or 1 vanilla pod, seeds scraped out)

250g ground almonds

150g coarse yellow polenta

1 ½ teaspoons baking powder

A good pinch of sea salt

Grated zest of 4 lemons

4 large eggs, beaten

Juice of 2 lemons (use the ones for zesting)

For the lemon syrup

Juice of 2 lemons (use the ones for zesting)

200g demerara sugar

Preheat the oven to 160°C/140°C fan/320°F/Gas mark 2 and line a 23 x 23 x 5cm tin with greaseproof paper.

Cream the butter and sugar together in a bowl with the vanilla until pale and fluffy.

Mix the almonds, polenta, baking powder, salt and lemon zest together in a separate bowl.

Slowly add the eggs to the butter mixture, with a handful of the dry ingredients to prevent the batter from curdling. Stir in the lemon juice and pour into the lined tin.

Bake for 1 hour – you may need to cover it with foil after 40 minutes to prevent the top becoming too brown.

Meanwhile, make the lemon syrup. Put the lemon juice and sugar in a pan over a medium heat and heat until the sugar has dissolved and the liquid has become syrupy.

Once the cake is cooked, remove it from the oven and slice into squares. Use a skewer to insert holes into the cake, then pour over the warm lemon syrup – you may not want to use all the syrup immediately, and I recommend reserving some for later.

Serve the slices warm with extra lemon syrup and crème fraîche.

Kenny's Crumble Cake

This was one of the first recipes I baked for the markets, given to me by my mother-in-law on a scrap of paper titled 'Kenny's crumble cake'. Kenny was a builder who converted my in-laws' old barn. It turns out this wasn't his recipe, but for a long time I thought it was. And I continue to joke with my wife that it probably is. Thank you, Kenny.

Serves 8

For the fruit

400g English rhubarb (or gooseberries, blackcurrants, blackberries, apricots, pears, apples or plums, depending on what's in season)

100g demerara sugar

Grated zest and juice of 1 unwaxed orange or well-scrubbed waxed orange

For the cake

200g unsalted butter

200g caster sugar

5 large eggs

265g self-raising flour

5½ tablespoons whole milk

A pinch of sea salt

For the crumble

80g unsalted butter

100g plain flour

100g demerara sugar

50g crushed hazelnuts or whole almonds

Firstly, prepare the fruit, which means peeling, stoning or trimming depending on what fruit you are using. Place the fruit in a bowl with the sugar and orange zest and juice. Leave it to rest for at least 1 hour.

Next, make the cake. Cream the butter and sugar together until pale and fluffy. Slowly add the eggs with a handful of flour to prevent the batter from curdling, then add the rest of the flour. Once all the egg and flour have been incorporated, stir in the milk and the salt.

For the crumble topping, use your fingertips to rub the butter and flour into large clumps (leaving large clumps creates a lovely rubbly texture), then stir in the sugar and nuts.

Preheat the oven to 180°C/160°C fan/350°F/Gas mark 4. Strain the fruit, reserving the excess juice. Grease and line a round 23cm loose-bottomed springform baking tin.

Spread half the cake batter over the base of the tin, followed by half the fruit. Add the remaining batter, followed by the rest of the fruit. Sprinkle the crumble topping over the fruit and press down slightly to compact.

Bake for 1 hour, or until a skewer inserted into the middle of the cake comes out clean.

Leave the crumble cake to rest for a few minutes before turning out onto a plate and slicing generously. Serve with custard or extra-thick double cream.

Tip: This is a tricky little cake to cut, which may mean you only get eight slices, but they will be hearty portions. Invest in a good sharp bread knife, and cut with real purpose.

Plum Crumble

The beauty of this crumble is that you can prepare the separate components in advance and bring them together 15 minutes before you need to serve. This method ensures the topping is still crunchy and alleviates any pre-dinner-party stress.

Serves 8–10

1 batch of Mr Pud's Poached Plums (see page 134) – about 1kg

2 batches of Kenny's Crumble Cake topping (see Tip, page 38)

Preheat the oven to 200°C/180°C fan/400°F/Gas mark mark 4.

Fill one large ovenproof dish or 8–10 smaller ovenproof dishes no more than two-thirds full with the compote, and set aside.

To make the crumble topping, use your fingertips to rub the butter and flour into large clumps (leaving large clumps creates a lovely rubbly texture), then stir in the sugar and hazelnuts. Spread the topping on to a baking tray lined with greaseproof paper and bake for 15 minutes until golden brown.

Remove from the oven and spoon the baked crumble topping over the compote, pressing down as you go. Return to the oven for a further 15 minutes, or until the fruit below is bubbling through. When ready, serve with custard or ice cream.

Tip: Any plums or crumble topping not required can be kept in the fridge or freezer for another day.

Poor Knights of Windsor

Who are these poor knights? They were a body of retired or impoverished knights founded by Edward III and provided with support and comfort in their final years – much like a modern-day Chelsea pensioner, perhaps. If I was in such a circumstance I know that the thought of this pudding would perk me up. Clarifying some butter (see Tip below) to fry with yields better results and reduces the likelihood that the poor knights will burn.

Serves 1

2 eggs, beaten

60ml full-fat milk

A shot of dark sherry (optional)

2 slices of brioche

1 tablespoon clarified butter (see Tip below)

Icing sugar

Greek yogurt and poached fruit (see pages 134–135), to serve

Whisk the eggs with the milk in a bowl, then stir in the sherry.

Soak both sides of the brioche in the milk mixture for 1–2 minutes per side.

Put a frying pan over a medium-high heat and add the clarified butter. When the butter starts to sizzle, add the soaked brioche and fry for 2–3 minutes on each side, or until golden brown. Before you turn the brioche over, dust a little icing sugar onto the surface of the brioche – this will help caramelise each side.

Remove from the pan and serve on a warmed plate with Greek yogurt and poached fruit. If having for brunch, you could add streaky bacon and maple syrup; or for pudding, serve with ice cream and chocolate sauce, maple syrup and pecans.

Tip: To clarify butter, take a whole pack of butter and heat it in a pan until it boils, then strain it through a jelly bag set over a bowl. You now have a stock of clarified butter to fry with. A generous teaspoon at a time will be enough.

Queen of Puddings

A pudding worthy of its name but one almost lost from modern life – perhaps due to its unsuitability for mass production or because the two main ingredients, custard and meringue, must be made fresh. Custard and meringue have both been victims of commercialisation and are more often bought ready-made for convenience. Either way, this pudding deserves to be reinstated on the throne – the layers of bread-enriched custard and jam all crowned with meringue are a perfect flavour and texture combination.

Serves 10

300g raspberry jam, warmed

For the custard

600ml double cream

4 large egg yolks

50g caster sugar

150g chunky breadcrumbs

For the meringue

4 large egg whites

275g caster sugar

Preheat the oven to 160°C/140°C fan/320°F/Gas mark 2.

First, make the custard. Add the cream to a heavy-based saucepan and heat gently over a low heat until almost boiled. Remove from the heat.

Whisk the egg yolks with the sugar in a bowl and pour over the warm cream mixture, whisking continuously, until just mixed.

Add the breadcrumbs to the base of a buttered 28cm x 5cm round ceramic pie dish and pour the custard over the top. Leave to rest for 15 minutes to allow the breadcrumbs to soak up the liquid.

Place the dish inside a deep baking tray and pour boiling water into the tray, until it is halfway up the dish. Bake for 25–30 minutes, until the custard has completely set. Remove from the oven and leave to cool slightly.

Meanwhile, make the meringue. Whisk the egg whites in a stand mixer on full speed until stiff peaks form. Add the caster sugar and 100ml of water to a saucepan and bring it to 120°C, testing the temperature with a sugar thermometer. Slowly pour the hot sugar syrup into the egg whites and continue to mix on maximum speed until stiff and shiny.

Spread the warmed jam over the cooled, set custard and pipe the meringue on top in lots of small individual peaks to form crowns (or simply spoon on top if preferred).

Increase the oven temperature to 180°C/160°C fan/350°F/Gas mark 4 and return the dish to the oven for about 25–30 minutes, until the meringue is golden and crisp. Serve hot with cream.

Sticky

Sticky Toffee Pudding

Steamed Treacle Sponge Pudding

Gingerbread Pudding

Steamed Paddington Pudding

Steamed Maple & Pecan Pudding

The Pudding Stop's Blueberry Roly Poly Slice

St Clement's Pond Pudding

Apple & Blackberry Eve's Pudding

Rum & Rasin Baba

Banana Spotted Dick

Plum & Stem Ginger Pudding

Verulam Pudding

Apple Upside Down Pudding

Aren't all puddings sticky? Well not necessarily, but warmth and stickiness are synonymous with a proper English pudding. Like many British bands, plenty of British puddings have struggled to make it in America. But as with the Beatles and the Rolling Stones, sticky toffee pudding is now as much a part of American life as it is ours. I think my recipe is as good as it gets and a few special tricks, like soaking the dates for long enough, adding espresso and pouring a little of the toffee sauce into the sponge as soon as the pudding is cooked, are all great tips for a top-notch toffee pud.

But of course there are others – and thank goodness, for sticky toffee pudding every day can become quite a bore. Take for example my Maple & Pecan Steamed Pudding, which combines everything I love about pecan pie, perched on a pert pillow of steamed sponge. Or my personal favourite, the Paddington Pudding. Named after my favourite childhood storybook character, Paddington Bear and our shared love of marmalade. This steamed sponge with a reservoir of homemade custard ready to be deployed on demand is just what I look forward to at 4 o'clock in the afternoon, knowing I have a cold few hours in the Pudmobile ahead of me.

Then there are the old classics; the less-fashionable ones that call for suet. They may have lost favour but they still have a strong following and are among the most delicious puddings. My Spotted Dick is updated with the addition of a banana, while the Roly Poly Pudding Slice encourages you to make you own blueberry jam – something you must try, as it's very simple and produces a roly poly that will remind what you've been missing since sitting down for school dinners.

Sticky Toffee Pudding

My first memory of this most English of puddings – believed to originate from the Lake District – was when my mum baked a big tray of it for cub camp. Every mother was asked to bring along food that would warm us up after a day of mud sliding and ice-cold showers. STP never failed to hit the spot! We'd eat it, saying sticky toffee pudding repeatedly as we did, getting our tongues tied. Sticky toffee pudding, sticky toffee pudding, stiffy tocky pudding, stocky tiffee pudding . . . Happy memories.

Serves 12

450g juicy Medjool dates, stoned

750ml water

3 teaspoons bicarbonate of soda

3 double shots of tasty espresso (from your local independent coffee shop if possible!)

160g unsalted butter

450g dark brown muscovado sugar

80g black treacle

3 large eggs

610g self-raising flour

A good pinch of sea salt

For the toffee sauce

260g dark brown muscovado sugar

140g black treacle

200g unsalted butter

300ml double cream

A pinch of sea salt

Add the dates and water to a saucepan over a medium heat and bring to the boil. Remove from the heat and add the bicarbonate of soda and espresso. Give the mixture a stir, place a lid on top and leave to soak for a few hours, or overnight. This time allows the dates to become soft and sticky, as the pudding should be.

Preheat the oven to 180°C/160°C fan/350°F/Gas mark 4, and line a 25 x 35 x 5cm baking dish with greaseproof paper.

In another pan, melt the butter, sugar and black treacle over a medium heat. Combine the flour and sea salt in a bowl.

Drain the date mixture, reserving the liquid, and add a little of the liquid to the butter and sugar mixture, which should by now be fully melted. Slowly whisk the flour into this mixture, until completely combined and there are no lumps. If the mixture becomes too stiff, add a little more of the cooking liquid to loosen. Once all the flour is incorporated, add the remaining cooking liquid and stir in the drained dates.

Pour the mixture into the prepared baking dish and bake for 35 minutes, until fully risen and springy to touch.

Meanwhile, make the sauce. Melt all the ingredients together in a saucepan over a medium heat, and whisk to combine. Bring to the boil, then take off the heat and set aside.

Once baked, remove from the oven, use a skewer to insert a few holes in the pudding, then pour over a little of the hot toffee sauce. Leave it to rest and soak for 5 minutes before portioning up and pouring more toffee sauce over the top to serve. I like to serve it with banana ice cream, which has the perfect toffee and banana 'banoffee' thing going on.

Steamed Treacle Sponge Pudding

My mother used to make an impromptu treacle sponge from scratch within 5 minutes of us finishing supper. She did cheat by using a microwave – but it was delicious, so we didn't care. This is an updated version that is less sweet and less microwaved.

Serves 4

100g golden syrup, plus extra, warmed, to serve

100g unsalted butter

100g light brown muscovado sugar

A pinch of sea salt

2 large eggs

100g self-raising flour

Grated zest of 1 lemon

1 teaspoon ground ginger

1 tablespoon black treacle

Pour the golden syrup into a 500ml pudding basin and place in the freezer while you make the sponge.

Cream the butter, sugar and salt in a bowl until light and fluffy. Slowly beat in the eggs, adding a handful of flour if the mixture shows any signs of curdling. Fold in the remaining flour, lemon zest, ginger and treacle.

Remove the pudding basin from the freezer and spoon the sponge mixture on top. Prepare the pudding for steaming (see page 13).

Place a large saucepan over a high heat, put the pudding inside and fill the pan halfway to two-thirds up the pudding basin with freshly boiled water. Quickly put a lid on and leave to steam for 1¼ hours, until it is springy to touch or a skewer inserted into the middle comes out clean.

When cooked, turn out onto a warm, large-rimmed plate and serve immediately with extra warmed syrup and custard or thick Jersey cream.

Gingerbread Pudding

This is a wonderful, warming recipe. It is really important to use a good-quality stem ginger and never be tempted to substitute the ginger syrup found within the jar for a bottle of that horrible stuff used to jazz up your gingerbread latte – it just won't taste the same.

Serves 8

350ml full-fat milk

150g dark brown muscovado sugar

1½ teaspoons bicarbonate of soda

75ml stem ginger syrup

150g unsalted butter

75g black treacle

150g golden syrup

275g self-raising flour

1½ tablespoons ground ginger

1 teaspoons ground cinnamon

1 teaspoons mixed spice

A pinch of sea salt

60g stem ginger, finely chopped

3 egg yolks

Butterscotch Sauce (page 213), to serve

Preheat the oven to 180°C/160°C fan/350°F/Gas mark 4.

Warm the milk and sugar in a heavy-based saucepan, and whisk to combine. Bring to a simmer, then remove from the heat and stir in the bicarbonate of soda. Stir in the stem ginger syrup.

Melt the butter, treacle and golden syrup in another large saucepan.

Sift the flour, spices and salt into a bowl. Add the stem ginger to the dry ingredients, using your fingers to rub it in and distribute it evenly.

You are now ready to combine all of the ingredients. Firstly, add a little of the milk mixture to the butter and treacle mixture to loosen, and whisk until smooth. Slowly begin to whisk the dry ingredients into this mixture, adding extra milk mixture to loosen when necessary. When all the flour has been incorporated, whisk in the remaining milk mixture and the egg yolks. The batter will be quite wet.

Pour the batter into a greased 25 x 5cm baking dish and bake for 40 minutes, or until the centre is springy to the touch.

Serve with warm butterscotch sauce and vanilla ice cream.

Steamed Paddington Pudding

Inspired by Paddington Bear's love of marmalade, this pudding combines two quintessentially English things – a steamed sponge and orange marmalade. Paddington Pudding gives everything you'd expect from the warm hug of a cuddly bear. Try to use bitter Seville orange marmalade – homemade and thick cut.

Serves 4

100g unsalted butter

100g light brown soft sugar

1 vanilla pod, split and seeds scraped out

Grated zest of 1 unwaxed orange

1 tablespoon black treacle

A pinch of sea salt

2 large eggs, beaten

100g self-raising flour

200g Seville marmalade, thickness of cut to your preference

Cream the butter, sugar and vanilla seeds in a bowl until pale and fluffy. To another bowl, add the orange zest, black treacle, salt and eggs. Very slowly add this mixture to the butter and sugar, pausing in between each addition to prevent the mixture from curdling, and adding a little flour if necessary. Fold in the rest of the flour.

Place 50g of marmalade into four individual 125ml pudding basins or ramekins and divide the batter between each pot. Prepare each pudding for steaming (see page 13). Place a large saucepan over a high heat, put the puddings inside and fill the pan halfway to two-thirds up the pudding basin with freshly boiled water. Steam for 30–40 minutes, or until the sponges are well risen and springy to touch. If necessary keep it topped up with more boiling water.

Alternatively, if you would like to make just one larger pudding, place the marmalade followed by the batter into a 500ml pudding basin, prepare for steaming (see page 13) and steam for 1½ hours.

Once cooked, turn the pudding out onto a warmed plate and serve with thick cream or custard.

Tip: These puddings can be kept for up to 3–4 days in the fridge and simply re-steamed to warm through.

Steamed Maple & Pecan Pudding

Maple syrup is such a wonderful natural bounty indigenous to North America. This pudding's combination of crunchy pecans, maple syrup and overtones of toffee, resting on a pert pillow of moist steamed sponge, make this a British/American 'special relationship' to remember.

Serves 8

75g pecan halves

200g unsalted butter

150g light brown soft sugar

1 vanilla pod, split and seeds scraped out

50g maple syrup

A pinch of sea salt flakes

4 large eggs

200g self-raising flour, sifted

For the maple and pecan topping

50g pecan nuts, lightly bashed

Maple syrup, for drizzling

Flaked sea salt (optional)

Line up eight 125ml plastic pudding basins with lids suitable for steaming on the work surface.

Sprinkle a few pecans into the bottom of each pudding basin, followed by a liberal squeeze of maple syrup and a pinch of flaked sea salt, if you are into that magical sweet and salty vibe.

Beat the butter and sugar in a bowl until pale and fluffy. Add the vanilla seeds, maple syrup and salt to the beaten eggs, then add this to the butter and sugar mix, a little at a time to prevent the mixture from curdling. Finally, fold in the flour and pecans.

Divide the batter between the basins and prepare each pudding for steaming (see page 13). Place a large saucepan over a high heat, put the pudding inside and fill the pan halfway to two-thirds up the pudding basin with freshly boiled water. Steam for 30–40 minutes, or until the sponges are well risen and springy to touch. If necessary keep the saucepan topped up with more boiling water.

Alternatively, if you would like to make just one larger pudding, place the pecans, maple syrup and salt followed by the sponge batter into a 1-litre pudding basin, prepare for steaming (see page 13) and steam for 1–1½ hours.

Once cooked, turn the puddings out into warmed bowls and served with extra maple syrup, thick cream, ice cream or custard in any combination you deem decadent and fulfilling.

Tip: This pudding can be kept for up to 3–4 days in the fridge and simply re-steamed to warm.

The Pudding Stop's Blueberry Roly Poly Slice

Beatrix Potter wrote *The Roly Poly Pudding*, a tale of childhood disobedience. Tabitha Twitchit locks Tom Kitten, her son, in the cupboard to keep him under control. However, he escapes and is captured by the rat Samuel Whiskers, who rolls him up in pastry to cook him as a roly poly pudding. Luckily, Mr Whiskers' plan is foiled when the other cats hear the commotion and come to Tom's rescue. Let it be a lesson to unruly children! When placing this pudding on the baking tray, make sure it fits well within it, as it will expand a lot as it cooks.

Makes 10–12 slices

2 batches of Suet Pastry (see page 24)

Self-raising flour, for dusting

1 batch of Simple Blueberry Jam (see page 224)

1 large egg, beaten

Preheat the oven to 200°C/180°C fan/400°F/Gas mark 6.

To construct your roly poly, roll out the suet pastry on a floured work surface to form a rectangle 10cm shorter in length than a 30 x 40cm baking tray. Spread the jam over the pastry, leaving a 2.5cm jam-free border. Brush the border with beaten egg.

Now you are ready to roll your pudding. Starting from the long side closest to you, very slowly roll up the pastry, using your hands to keep each roll very tight to the previous one. As you get to the final roll, work towards moving the roly poly so that the final seam is on the bottom of the pudding.

Cut pieces of greaseproof paper and foil of equal size, and big enough to wrap the pudding up loosely like a parcel – the pudding will expand in the oven, so to constrict it by wrapping too tightly would mean that the pudding may not be as light as it should be.

Place the paper directly on top of the foil, and the pudding seam side down in the middle. Wrap up loosely like a big cracker, twisting both ends and folding over the foil a few times where it meets all the way along the top of the pudding.

Place the wrapped pudding on a roasting rack set on a roasting tin and fill the tin two-thirds high with freshly boiled water. Bake for 50 minutes to 1 hour, or until it is well risen and slightly golden on top.

When cooked, carefully remove from the oven and place the pudding on a large board to rest for 10 minutes or so.

Carefully unwrap the pudding. You can either slice the pudding into portions at this point or, if you're proud of your pudding, transfer it to a large serving plate and serve at the table with a dusting of icing sugar and a big jug of custard.

St Clement's Pond Pudding

A pond pudding, like a chocolate fondant, has this clever trick of revealing a lovely little sauce. Unlike a fondant, though, a pond pudding's sauce comes from lots of cooking, as opposed to undercooking. Sussex is credited with being the origin of the pond pudding, distinguished by containing a whole lemon. The lemon cooks slowly and candies itself, encased by a rich suet crust. Once cooked, and once the suet crust is breached, lovely lemony nectar reveals itself. A pudding that is self-saucing is a very convenient pudding indeed.

Serves 4–6

250g self-raising flour

A pinch of sea salt

1 teaspoon baking powder

zest of 1 unwaxed orange

100g suet

100ml buttermilk

100ml water

100g cold butter, diced

50g light brown soft sugar

1 unwaxed lemon

1 vanilla pod, split and seeds scraped out

50g honey

Mix the flour, salt, baking powder, orange zest and suet in a bowl. Mix the buttermilk and water in a separate bowl, then slowly pour this into the dry ingredients, mixing until the mixture has formed a soft dough that is easy to handle using your hands or a spoon – you may not need all the wet ingredients.

Roll out the dough to a circle 7.5cm wider than the diameter of a 1-litre pudding basin. Cut out a quarter section of the dough and set aside – this will be used later for the lid. Carefully use the remaining rolled-out pastry to line the pudding basin, pressing the sides together to seal.

Put half the butter and all the sugar on top of the pastry. Spike the lemon all over with a larding needle (or a big skewer) to allow the juices to escape, and place the lemon on top of the butter and sugar. Add the remaining butter, the vanilla and the honey.

Roll out the reserved pastry and place on top to make a lid, sealing carefully to ensure no juices escape during steaming.

Prepare the pudding for steaming (see page 13). Place a large saucepan over a high heat, put the pudding inside and fill the pan halfway to two-thirds up the pudding basin with freshly boiled water. Quickly put a lid on and leave to boil for 4 hours. If necessary keep it topped up with more boiling water.

Once cooked, leave the pudding to rest for a few moments. Remove the foil lid, run a butter knife around the edge of the pudding and invert it onto a large plate. Let the pond reveal itself, and serve immediately with cold cream.

Apple & Blackberry Eve's Pudding

Adam and Eve eating a forbidden apple from the tree in the Garden of Eden and the subsequent 'Fall of Man' is one of the most famous stories from Christian theology. This 'Fall of Man' purportedly bought sin to the world – and a world without sin would be a world without Eve's pudding. What a shame that would be. Amen.

Serves 6–8

A large knob of butter

4 tablespoons caster sugar

500g Bramley apples, peeled, cored and roughly chopped

Grated zest of 1 lemon

250g blackberries

For the sponge

175g butter

175g caster sugar

A pinch of sea salt

1 vanilla pod, split and seeds scraped out

3 large eggs

250g self-raising flour

3 tablespoons full-fat milk

A handful of flaked almonds

Preheat the oven to 180°C/160°C fan/350°F/Gas mark 4 and grease a round 28 x 5cm round ovenproof dish.

First, make the sponge. Cream the butter, sugar, salt and vanilla seeds together until pale and fluffy. Slowly add the eggs, one at a time, to prevent the mixture from curdling. Fold in the flour and stir in the milk.

Put a saucepan over a moderate heat and, when hot, add the butter and sugar and melt until foaming. Add the apples and the lemon zest. Cook for 5 minutes until the apples have started to break down a little. Remove from the heat and stir in the blackberries.

Transfer the mixture to the greased dish. Pour the sponge batter over the apples and blackberries, sprinkle with almonds and bake for 30–35 minutes, until lightly golden and the sponge springs back when touched. Serve immediately with custard.

Rum & Raisin Baba

Rum ba-ba, rum ba-ba. Have you any more? Yes sir, yes sir. Three jars full.

The rum baba is a butter-enriched bun attributed to Paris, introduced by an exiled king of Poland (where the *babka* originates) who re-invigorated his dry baba with liquor after a long voyage. In Britain, the rum baba became synonymous with 1970s retro puddings together with the Arctic roll, Black Forest gateau and Angel Delight. I like my baba hot from the oven, dunked in the rum-laced syrup with a scoop of ice cream. But they are also very good left to cool and steep in the rum syrup contained within a sterilised, sealed Kilner jar.

Makes 8 babas

1 tablespoon light brown soft sugar

75g strong white bread flour

25g white spelt flour

A pinch of sea salt flakes

20g fresh yeast or 5g fast-action yeast

2 large eggs, gently beaten

50g unsalted butter, softened and diced

40g raisins

For the syrup

250g caster sugar

250ml water

175ml rum

Combine the sugar and both the flours in the bowl of a stand mixer. Add the salt and yeast to opposite sides of the bowl. Turn the mixer on at a low speed and gradually add the beaten eggs. Once fully combined, start to add half the butter, a few pieces at a time. Continue to add the remaining butter until it has all been incorporated. You should end up with a really glossy and elastic dough. Add the raisins and mix to distribute evenly.

Use a couple of teaspoons to divide the dough into an 8-hole, 7cm diameter well-greased muffin tin. Leave the buns to prove for 1 hour in a warm place, or until the buns fill their holes. Preheat the oven to 220°C/200°C fan/425°F/Gas mark 7 and bake for 13 minutes.

Meanwhile, make the syrup. Dissolve the sugar in the water in a large saucepan. Place over a medium heat and bring to the boil. Leave to boil for 3–5 minutes, then remove from the heat and add the rum. Set aside.

Check on your babas – they are baked when they have risen above the muffin tin and are golden brown on top. Remove from the oven and turn out onto a wire rack to cool.

How to serve the buns is your choice, as they are equally good served warm or cold. To serve warm, place a bun in a warmed bowl and pour over 90ml of the warm rum syrup. Serve with ice cream or a dollop of extra-thick cream. You can store the babas in a sterilised Kilner jar with the remaining rum syrup for up to 2 weeks.

Banana Spotted Dick

Is a spotted dick the most famous English pudding and double entendre known? Possibly. Spotted dick is traditionally one of the less-sweet English puddings, with sweetness coming from the 'spotted' currants and mandatory custard. Bananas add a little more natural sweetness, and bananas with custard is just wow.

Serves 6

200g self-raising flour

1 teaspoon baking powder

100g shredded suet

50g caster sugar

2 teaspoons ground cinnamon

A pinch of sea salt

1 egg yolk

100ml buttermilk

300g really ripe bananas, chopped

150g currants

Butter, for greasing

Sift the flour and the baking powder into a large bowl and add the suet, sugar, cinnamon and salt. Add the egg yolk to the buttermilk and mix well with the dry ingredients. Add the bananas and currants and squish with your hands to combine.

Transfer the spotted dick to a greased 500ml pudding basin and push down to evenly distribute. Prepare the pudding for steaming (see page 13).

Place a large saucepan over a high heat, put the pudding inside and fill the pan halfway to two-thirds up the pudding basin with freshly boiled water. Quickly put a lid on and leave to boil for 1½ hours. Keep the water topped up with more boiling water if necessary. The pudding is done when it has risen fully and is firm to touch.

Remove the pudding from the pan, and leave to rest before turning out onto a plate. Serve immediately with a large jug of hot custard.

Plum & Stem Ginger Pudding

This is a really simple recipe which shows how easy it is to create your own pudding by following a few basic rules: 1. Take a simple sponge recipe; 2. Pick flavour combinations that work; 3. Add some texture; 4. Cook it perfectly; 5. Serve it with custard. Simple!

For this pudding the sponge is a typical 1:1:1 butter, sugar, flour ratio with enough eggs to hold the batter together. Fragrant plums with the piquancy of stem ginger are made for each other – adding incredible flavour and texture. Options to modify further can come from using a different type of sugar or fresh fruit, adding ground spices, zest of fruit, dried fruit and so on.

Serves 6

100g unsalted butter, plus extra for greasing

100g self-raising flour, plus extra for dusting

100g light brown soft sugar

2 large eggs

A pinch of salt

75ml stem ginger syrup

60g stem ginger, coarsely grated

4 large English Victoria plums, stoned and quatered

1 tablespoon plain flour

Preheat the oven to 180°C/160°C fan/350°F/Gas mark 4. Grease six 175ml dariole moulds with butter, then dust with flour and tap down to remove any excess flour.

Cream the butter and sugar together in a bowl until pale and fluffy. Slowly add the eggs, then the self-raising flour and the salt. Stir in the ginger syrup.

Place the plain flour in a separate bowl and add the stem ginger and sliced plums. Give the plum and ginger a gentle mix before adding them to the batter. Divide among the dariole moulds, ensuring that each has an even amount of plum and ginger pieces.

Bake for 30 minutes, until each pudding has risen and is starting to turn golden brown. Remove from the oven and leave to stand for a few moments. Run a knife around the inside of each mould before turning out into bowls. Serve immediately with butterscotch sauce and ice cream or custard.

Tip: Other combinations that work include rhubarb and ginger, rhubarb and cardamom, plum and star anise, apple and cinnamon, and pear and chocolate chips. Feel free to use milk to replace the ginger syrup where appropriate.

Verulam Pudding

The story goes something like this. In the eight century a monk at St Albans monastery wanted to feed the poor on Good Friday with a wholesome bun. He came up with what we now know as the hot cross bun. The only difference was his addition of cardamom, or 'seeds of paradise', and slashes rather than a piped cross topping. This is a take on the classic bread and butter pudding, and is a great way to use up old hot cross buns. Verulam is the ancient roman name for St Albans, and Verulam Road the street on which The Pudding Stop lives.

Serves 8

250ml full-fat milk

250ml double cream

6 cardamom pods, bashed up

6 egg yolks

70g caster sugar

50g raisins

Butter, softened, for spreading

1 x 450g jar of orange marmalade, warmed, to glaze

6–8 hot cross buns, at least a day old, split in half

Pour the milk, cream and cardamom into a heavy-based saucepan and place over a medium heat. Bring the mixture to the boil, then remove from the heat, put to one side and leave to cool to room temperature before passing through a sieve to remove the cardamom.

Whisk the egg yolks and sugar in a bowl. Pour the cardamom-infused cream mixture onto the eggs and whisk until combined.

Grease a 25 x 35 x 5cm ceramic pie dish, and scatter the raisins over the bottom of the dish. Liberally butter and marmalade the split hot cross buns. Lay them in the dish, buttered side up, overlapping slightly, until they reach the top. Pour the custard mixture over the buns and leave to soak in for 20 minutes. You may not need all the custard at first. But after 20 minutes, and if there is room, add a little more custard. If you still have some custard left over you can add it back to a saucepan and cook it as normal and serve it along side the pudding. Preheat the oven to 120°C/100°C fan/240°F/Gas mark ½.

Place the dish in a deep roasting tin and pour boiling water into the tin until it comes halfway up the pudding dish. Bake for 30 minutes, until the custard is cooked. Remove from the oven and leave the pudding to settle for 10 minutes before serving with ice cream, cream or custard.

Apple Upside Down Pudding

I like to use Bramleys here as they're the perfect dessert apple – slightly sour, ready to counter a pudding's sweetness, and turning golden and fluffy when cooked. A whole baked Bramley stuffed with dried fruit and sugar through its core is a jolly good option for anyone on a dairy-free diet. However, this upside down cake is an even better option – especially if served with my Brown Sugar Almond Custard (see page 221).

Makes 6 individual puddings

300g Bramley apples, peeled, cored and diced

175g light brown soft sugar

150g ground almonds

50g coarse polenta

1 teaspoon baking powder

Grated zest of 1 orange

1 teaspoon mixed spiced 4 large eggs

6 tablespoons maple or golden syrup

Place the apples in a pan with a splash of water and cook over a gentle heat until soft. Remove from the heat and leave to cool. Put 75g aside to decorate the puddings.

Once fully cool, add 225g apples to a food processor or blender and blend until smooth. Add the sugar, almonds, polenta, baking powder, orange zest and mixed spice to the food processor, and blend until smooth. With the machine still running, add one egg at a time. After the final addition, blend for a minute or so, then set aside.

Place a tablespoon of syrup at the bottom of each pudding basin, followed by the leftover apple and spoon the batter on top. Prepare the puddings for steaming (see page 13).

Secure the lid on each pudding basin and place in a large saucepan with enough boiling water in the pan to come two-thirds of the way up each pudding. Steam with the lid on for up to 1 hour, or until each pudding is risen and springy to touch.

Remove the puddings from the steamer and turn out onto plates. Serve with the Brown Sugar Almond Custard to keep it dairy-free.

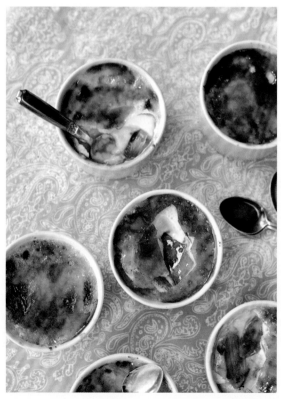

Creamy

Custard Tart

Tayberry Cranachan

New York Cheesecake

Proper English Trifle

Rhubarb Burnt Cream

Yorkshire Curd Cheesecake

Buttermilk Pudding

Pedro's Rice Pudding

Everlasting Apple Cider Syllabub

Portuguese Custard Tarts

Banana & Butterscotch Soufflé

You might wonder how I can include a whole chapter on creamy pudding alone. Surely creamy is creamy? Alas, the remarkable thing is that there is a scale of creaminess and texture, and as on any good scale there are degrees of light and shade. This chapter includes classics from home and abroad, from New York cheesecake to rhubarb burnt cream, syllabub, posset and soufflé.

The type of creaminess does vary significantly from one pud to the next – especially when other textures are added. And texture such as a crunchy or melting pastry, or a biscuit base, or a nice bit of shortbread to dunk is a lovely addition to any creamy filling. A New York cheesecake will stick to the roof of your mouth, while a burnt cream will melt on your tongue. An English custard tart with the same texture as a burnt cream will be completely different against the soft melting nature of shortcrust pastry versus the brittle crunch of burnt sugar. Then there's rice pudding – no less enjoyable than a silky set custard, just different. And what about a wobbly gelatinous creamy pudding like panna cotta, or a jelly-heavy trifle layered with creamy custard? All brilliant creamy puddings and very different, despite essentially containing the same ingredients of eggs, sugar and cream.

So there you are – make them all – line them up, invite some friends over and celebrate creamy puddings.

Custard Tart

Custard tart is a classic English dessert dating back to medieval times – featuring at the coronation of King Henry IV in 1399. Often, the cream was substituted for almond milk during Lent by the wealthy. I suggest adding a twist to the tart by flavouring the custard with bergamot, the flavour of Earl Grey tea. Earl Grey was established by a jealous English tea merchant imitating more expensive Chinese teas in the nineteenth century. I can't help thinking that the Chinese may now be jealous of this custard tart.

Serves 10

350g Sweet Pastry (see page 21)

Flour, for dusting

7 large egg yolks

625g double cream

8 Earl Grey tea bags or 1 vanilla pod, split and seeds scraped out (optional)

75g caster sugar

1 whole nutmeg

Roll out the pastry on a lightly floured work surface to about 3mm thick. Use it to line a greased 23cm loose-bottomed tart tin, prick all over with a fork and chill for 30 minutes. Preheat the oven to 180°C/160°C fan/350°F/Gas mark 4.

Line the pastry shell with foil and fill with baking beans. Bake for about 15 minutes, until golden brown around the edges. Remove the foil and baking beans and return the pastry case to the oven for 1–2 minutes, until it is a good golden brown colour all over.

Lightly beat one of the egg yolks, remove the pastry case from the oven and brush egg all over the inside of the pastry case to seal. Return it to the oven for 1 more minute, then remove and leave to cool. Lower the oven temperature to 120°C/100°C fan/250°F/Gas mark ½ .

For the custard, put the cream and the Earl Grey tea bags or vanilla, if using, in a heavy-based saucepan with half of the sugar. Bring to the boil over a medium-high heat. If using the tea bags, strain the mixture through a fine sieve into a bowl, squeezing the tea bags gently in the sieve.

Whisk the remaining egg yolks with the remaining sugar in another bowl, then slowly pour over the warm double cream and whisk together. Pass the mixture through a fine sieve into a jug.

Place the pastry case in the oven, leaving enough space above to pour from the jug. Pour the custard into the pastry case and grate nutmeg liberally all over. Bake for 50–55 minutes, until there is a gentle wobble in the centre of the tart. Remove from the oven and place the tin on a rack to cool. Leave to cool completely, then serve with a cup of Chinese tea.

Tayberry Cranachan

The tayberry is a cross between a blackberry and a raspberry, named after the River Tay in Scotland. If you don't happen to live near a tayberry bush, raspberries or blackberries, or a mixture of both, are equally tasty.

Serves 2-3

160g rolled oats

3 tablespoons Scotch single malt whisky

500ml double cream

8 tablespoons honey

A handful of raspberries or blackberries

Soak the rolled oats overnight in the whisky.

Whip the cream with the honey and stir in the whisky-laced oats, along with a handful of raspberries or blackberries. You can loosen with extra whisky if you find the mixture is a little dry.

New York Cheesecake

Cheesecake is a universal dessert from every corner of the world. There are many forms, differentiated by the cheese used and whether they are baked or not. Ricotta, quark, curd and cream cheese all yield different results. Many English cheesecake recipes have been found from the fourteenth century, and typically contained dried fruits and spices and were always baked. Yorkshire curd tart is essentially a cheesecake containing curd cheese, allspice and dried fruit baked inside pastry. A New York cheesecake is characterised by the addition of soured or double cream, making it rich, dense and creamy. Bake at a high temperature to achieve that wonderful golden top.

Serves 8–10

65g butter

200g ginger biscuits

1 teaspoon ground ginger

25g demerara sugar

For the filling

500g full-fat cream cheese

200g soured or double cream

120g caster sugar

1 vanilla pod, split and seeds scraped out

3 tablespoons plain flour

4 large eggs

Preheat the oven to 180°C/160°C fan/350°F/Gas mark 4 and grease and line a 23cm springform tin.

First, make the cheesecake base. Melt the butter in a saucepan. Put the ginger biscuits in a food processor and blend to fine crumbs. Stir the biscuit crumbs into the melted butter and add the ground ginger and sugar.

Press the mixture into the tin with the back of a teaspoon and bake for 10–15 minutes, or until golden brown.

For the filling, whisk the cream cheese, soured cream, sugar, vanilla seeds and flour in a large bowl. Once the mixture is thick and well combined, slowly whisk in the eggs.

Remove the biscuit base from the oven, and pour in the cheesecake filling. Reduce the oven temperature to 160°C/140°C fan/320°F/Gas mark 2. Return the cheesecake to the oven for 45 minutes, or until a wobble remains in the centre and the top is golden brown.

At this point turn the oven off, but leave the cheesecake inside with the door open until it has cooled. This will prevent it from cracking.

Proper English Trifle

'It is, of course, a trifle, but there is nothing so important as trifles.'
Sherlock Holmes

There is simply no finer example of an English pudding than a trifle. It combines components that when eaten alone would surely be satisfying enough. I mean custard, yum. Jelly, double yum. Jam and sponge soaked in sherry, triple yum. I could go on . . .

Serves 4–6

1 batch of sponge (see Eve's Pudding on page 64) baked in a 900g loaf tin

A jar of good-quality strawberry jam

4–6 tablespoons dry sherry

1 batch of Strawberry & Rhubarb Jelly (see page 154)

1 batch of Custard (see page 216)

4 batches Vanilla Cream (see page 223)

Flaked almonds, lightly toasted

Slice the sponge cake into thumb-width slices. Spread one side of each piece with jam and arrange over the base of a trifle dish. Drizzle the sherry over the sponge, aiming to coat all of it but showing some restraint – 4–6 tablespoons should be enough.

Make the Strawberry & Rhubarb Jelly as instructed on page 154 and at the point that you would pour into a jelly mould, pour directly onto the sponge. Place in the fridge to allow the jelly to set. Preheat the oven to 200°C/180°C fan/400°F/Gas mark 6.

While the jelly is setting, ensure you have your custard made and chilled as well as your vanilla cream.

For the almonds, place 2–3 generous handfuls on a clean roasting tray and bake for 10–12 minutes, or until they are golden brown. Leave to cool.

Once the jelly is fully set (you can test this by poking it with your finger!) and you have all your elements ready to go, you can start assembling. Remove the trifle dish from the fridge and spoon the custard on top of the jelly, followed by the vanilla cream, shaping it like the dome of St Paul's cathedral. Finish with liberal sprinkles of your toasted almonds, then take it proudly to the table with plenty of glass bowls and the biggest spoon you own.

Rhubarb Burnt Cream

When it comes to the aetiology of British puddings, Cambridge burnt cream has all the drama, humour and irony of a Hollywood blockbuster. The basic plot involves a French cook visiting England in the seventeenth century, and stumbling across a Cambridge college cook baking lovely custards with a caramelised sugar crust. He heads back to France to publish the recipe for crème brûlée – the direct translation of burnt cream. That French classic is based on none other than this humble English pud. And what's more English than rhubarb and custard?

Makes 6

300g Yorkshire forced rhubarb, cut into 2.5cm batons

50g light brown soft sugar

650ml double cream

1 vanilla pod, split and seeds scraped out

10 large egg yolks

100g caster sugar, plus 6 teaspoons for the topping

Preheat the oven to 160°C/140°C fan/320°F/Gas mark 2.

Put a saucepan over a medium heat and add the rhubarb, light brown soft sugar and 1 tablespoon of water. Leave the rhubarb to cook slowly for 10–15 minutes, until softened. Check the sweetness – you want to leave the rhubarb a little tart to offset the sweet custard.

Put the cream and the vanilla seeds in a heavy-based saucepan, and bring to the boil over a medium heat.

Whisk the egg yolks with the caster sugar in a large bowl until well combined. Once the cream has reached boiling point, carefully pour it into the bowl of eggs and sugar, whisking continuously. Pass the mixture through a sieve into a jug.

Spread the rhubarb among six 175ml ramekins, then gently pour the custard on top. Put the ramekins in a deep roasting tin and pour boiling water into the tin until the water is halfway up each ramekin. Bake for 35–40 minutes, until only a slight wobble remains. Remove from the oven and leave to cool fully before placing in the fridge for at least 2 hours before serving.

When ready to serve, sprinkle a teaspoon of caster sugar over the tops of each baked custard and place under a hot grill until the sugar has caramelised. Alternatively, you can use a blowtorch.

Yorkshire Curd Cheesecake

This is a pastry-free version of Yorkshire curd tart – it is therefore a cheesecake, and flour-free. The addition of spice and lemon zest lifts the naturally tangy curd, and the dried fruit plumps up nicely as the curd releases its natural juices. Rosewater was often added to Yorkshire curd tarts, but if you buy a really good quality curd, then I say let it sing!

Serves 10–12

1kg curd cheese (sheep's, cow's, goat's, lemur's or whatever you can get your hands on)

250g caster sugar

6 eggs, beaten

Grated zest and juice of 1 lemon

¼ teaspoon ground allspice

¼ tsp ground nutmeg

100g dried fruit (currants, prunes, raisins or sultanas all work well)

Preheat the oven to 160°C/140°C fan/320°F/Gas mark 2 and line a 23cm cake tin with greaseproof paper.

Very gently whisk the curd with the sugar in a bowl. Gradually add the beaten eggs, whisking well between each addition. Stir in the lemon, spices and dried fruit.

Pour into the lined cake tin and bake for 40–50 minutes until golden on top. Leave to cool completely and serve with a spoonful of Pedro-Pimped Prunes (see page 226).

Buttermilk Pudding

Buttermilk is a by-product of churning butter from cream. It has a slightly sour taste and brings great flavour to this pudding, which is what the Italians call panna cotta – or cooked cream. You can make your own buttermilk by whisking double cream until you're left with a clump of homemade butter in the whisk and buttermilk in the bowl. Alternatively, you can pick it up from any high street store.

Makes 8 puddings

25g bronze leaf gelatine

360ml full-fat milk

360ml double cream

1 vanilla pod, split and seeds scraped out

180g caster sugar

520ml buttermilk

1 ½ teaspoons lemon juice

Soak the gelatine leaves in cold water until soft, then squeeze out the excess water and set aside.

Pour the milk and cream into a saucepan with the vanilla seeds, and bring to the boil. Remove from the heat and leave to infuse. When the mixture reaches blood temperature, whisk the sugar into the warm milk and cream, followed by the gelatine.

When the mixture reaches room temperature, stir in the buttermilk and lemon juice, then pass through a fine sieve into a jug.

Divide the buttermilk pudding between eight 175ml dariole moulds and leave in the fridge for at least a few hours to set, although they are best left overnight, as the flavour will improve over the next day or so.

To remove the puddings, dip the base of each dariole mould in warm water. After a few moments you'll be able to pull the pudding away from the sides with your fingers. At this point invert the pudding onto a flat plate, shake, and the pudding should drop out. Carefully remove the moulds and serve with stewed fruit and shortbread.

Pedro's Rice Pudding

If you take a bottle of dark and sticky Pedro Ximenez sherry and cover a tub full of prunes, after a week or so you will have nice plump, sweet, Pedro-Pimped Prunes (see page 226). These prunes are your new best friend, and can be served with cheesecake, custard tart or any creamy pudding. They also happen to work brilliantly with rice pudding. Lovely jubbly.

Serves 6–8

100g short-grain rice

50g caster sugar

600ml full-fat milk

600ml double cream

1 vanilla pod, split and seeds scraped out

Grated nutmeg, to taste

Approximately 20 Pedro-Pimped Prunes without the syrup (see page 226)

A couple of knobs of butter

Preheat the oven to 120°C/100°C fan/250°F/Gas mark ½.

Put all the ingredients in 28 x 5cm round ovenproof dish, finishing with a few knobs of butter and some grated nutmeg on top. Dot Pedro-Pimped Prunes into the mixture – as many as you like.

Bake for 1½–2 hours, stirring only once. The secret to getting this pudding right is cooking it on a low heat and very slowly. Serve with an extra spoonful of Pedro-pimped Prunes and some extra-thick double cream.

Everlasting Apple Cider Syllabub

The syllabub features infrequently on restaurant menus of the twenty-first century – replaced by ice cream as a refreshing end to a meal. Originally a syllabub was fresh-from-the-cow milk directed into a bowl of cider or wine. The light curd was left to separate from the whey, which remained at the bottom. People used special spouted glasses – slurping the whey through the spout and then eating the frothy curds with a spoon. Over time a thickening agent such as gelatine was used, resulting in an everlasting syllabub – a thicker and richer syllabub that could be kept in a glass for hours or overnight before serving. This syllabub's texture is much like the posset of today.

Serves 4

200g Bramley apples, peeled, cored and diced

1 clove

1 allspice berry

1 cinnamon stick

1 whole nutmeg, grated

75g caster sugar

100ml dry cider

300ml double cream

Place the apples in a pan with a splash of water and cook over a gentle heat until soft. Remove from the heat and leave to cool.

Bash the whole spices in a pestle and mortar to help them release their flavour.

Set aside some nutmeg for the garnish. Combine the bashed spices, remaining nutmeg, sugar and cider in a bowl and leave to steep for at least 1 hour or preferably overnight. Strain through a muslin cloth into a clean bowl.

Slowly pour the double cream into the strained mixture in a continuous stream, whisking all the time, until the mixture thickens. The cream mixture must just hold its shape when the whisk is lifted.

Spoon a couple of tablespoons of the stewed apples into four glasses and pour the cider syllabub on top. You're are aiming for roughly one part apple to two parts syllabub. Chill for several hours, dust with nutmeg and serve with a glass of warmed cider and shortbread.

Portuguese Custard Tarts

These famous little tarts, pastéis de nata, were baked at a monastery in Lisbon around the eighteenth century to use up egg yolks discarded by nuns starching their clothes with the whites. Over time they sold these pastries to generate revenue in a bid to hold off impending closure – in the end the monastery did close and the recipe was sold to the ancestors who still own the world-famous Pastéis de Belém today. This recipe needs to be started the day before.

Makes 12 tarts

1 batch of Quick Puff Pastry (see page 23)

For the custard

500ml double cream

300ml full-fat milk

2 vanilla pods, split and seeds scraped out

8 egg yolks (use the whites to make pavlova on page 148)

4 tablespoons plain flour

250g caster sugar

First, make the custard. Put the cream, milk and split vanilla pod and seeds in a saucepan over a medium heat. Bring to the boil, then set aside.

Whisk the egg yolks, flour and caster sugar in a large bowl, until you have a thick paste. Slowly pour the hot liquid onto this mixture, whisking continuously, until all the ingredients are combined. Return the mixture back to the pan over a medium heat and cook slowly until the custard thickens to the consistency of mayonnaise – do not stop whisking or turn the heat up too high, or the custard will split.

Once your custard is sufficiently thick, remove from the heat and pour into a cold, clean bowl. Keep whisking until the custard has cooled – this prevents the custard from curdling.

Once cooled, pour the custard into a lidded lunchbox or bowl covered with cling film and chill overnight. This custard can be kept for 2–3 days in the fridge.

The next day, roll out the pastry on a floured work surface to about 3mm thick in a large rectangle. Roll the pastry up from the longest end closest to you. Keep each turn as tight as possible as you roll, as this will create more layers within the pastry. Once rolled up into a long sausage, cut into 5cm-wide batons (each baton should weigh 30g).

Take a 5cm baton, turn it cut-side down, and roll out to a size that allows you to line the bottom and sides of the 7cm diameter holes in a muffin tin. Repeat until you've lined the holes in your tin. Prick the base of each tart shell with a fork.

continues overleaf ...

Preheat the oven to its highest setting, preferably to 250°C/230°C fan/500°F/Gas mark 9 with low or no fan. Spoon 1½ tablespoons of custard into each tart shell, or until three-quarters full, and chill in the fridge for 10 minutes, by which time the oven should be hot enough.

Place the tarts on the top shelf of the oven and bake for 7–9 minutes, until the pastry is golden brown and the custard has a mottled golden brown colour. The tarts will keep for 1–2 days and are best served at room temperature.

Banana & Butterscotch Soufflé

A soufflé must have texture on the inside and the outside. There are a few basic rules that are essential to follow for the perfect soufflé. The custard and puréed fruit base provide the flavour, and the egg white the lift. Baking a soufflé at a high temperature for a short time creates a crispy golden outside and a gooey inside. Soufflé means to 'puff up' – remember, if you knock the air out of your whites, it will not soufflé.

Serves 8

5 ripe bananas

A dash of lemon juice

Melted butter, for brushing

75g caster sugar, plus extra to dust

4 large egg whites

A pinch of salt

Icing sugar, to dust

For the creme patissiere

200ml full-fat milk

150ml double cream

1 vanilla pod, split and seeds scraped out

4 large egg yolks

60g caster sugar

10g cornflour

15g plain flour

Preheat the oven to 190°C/170°C fan/375°F/Gas mark 5.

Begin by making the crème patissiere. Put the milk, cream and split vanilla pod and scraped seeds in a heavy-based saucepan and bring to the boil. Remove from the heat and leave the vanilla to infuse.

Whisk the egg yolks and sugar together in a large bowl. Sift the cornflour and plain flour together in another bowl. Add the sifted flours to the egg mixture and combine.

Slowly pour the warm milk and cream mixture into the bowl, whisking continuously. Once fully combined, return to the saucepan and cook over a medium heat, stirring continuously, until the custard is thick and can coat a spoon. Set aside and cover with cling film to prevent a skin from forming.

Peel the bananas and put them in a food processor or blender. Add a dash of lemon juice, then blend until smooth. Add this to the crème patissiere and cover.

Prepare eight soufflé dishes by brushing liberally with butter using upward strokes. Dust the insides with caster sugar, then tap out any excess.

Whisk the egg whites with a pinch of salt in a large bowl, until soft peaks form. Slowly add the caster sugar a teaspoon at a time until you have achieved a smooth and glossy meringue.

continues overleaf ...

To assemble the soufflé, whisk one-third of the meringue into the banana custard mixture then, using a large metal spoon, fold in the rest until well combined. Be very careful – if you over-beat the mixture, the air will escape and the soufflés will not have beautifully raised golden hats.

Pour the mixture into the soufflé dishes, tap the dishes on the work surface and smooth off the tops with a palette knife. Ensure the top of the dishes, both inside and outside, are completely clean and free of batter – if not, the soufflé will stick and will not rise evenly.

Bake for 10–12 minutes, until nicely risen and golden brown on top. Do not open the oven until this point, or the souffles will collapse. Remove from the oven, dust liberally with icing sugar and serve immediately with a jug of warmed butterscotch sauce and cold pouring cream.

Fruity

Strawberry & Peanut Butter Crumble

Gooseberry & Elderflower Suet Pudding

Apricot Tarte Tatin

Apple & Bilberry Pie

Apricot & Raspberry Crumble

Baked Summer Pudding

Cherry Pie

Lemon Tart (& Lemon Meringue Pie)

Spiced Nectarine Tart

Rhubarb Charlotte

Buttermilk Pancakes

Aside from serving crowd-pleasing classics such as sticky toffee pudding, spotted dick and ginger pudding all year round – it is the puddings that include seasonal fruits that inspire our changing menu at The Pudding Stop. Crumbles and steamed sponges feature on our menu throughout the year, but a crumble in early summer featuring apricots or strawberries will be very different to an apple and blackberry crumble come early autumn. Similarly, a steamed pudding with a homemade Seville orange marmalade from its short season at the beginning of the year will move to a blueberry jam steamed sponge when blueberries peak at the height of the British summer.

It has been mentioned so often, and by so many, how lucky we are to live on these British Isles with a seasonally changing bounty of natural produce to pick from. And it doesn't just apply to fruits. Nuts follow the seasons too – I really look forward to chestnuts at Christmas and cobnuts in the autumn.

Finally, I urge you to experiment and create your own recipes and flavour combinations once you have tried mine. Use my recipes as a guide to help you play around with different fruits. Try apple and plum pie, or a plum tart instead of apricot tart, or a blueberry pie instead of cherry. When substituting fruits, ensure you pick a fruit with a similar structure and texture and you won't go wrong. Remember that you can always adjust the sweetness with a little more or less sugar or a liberal squeeze of honey or maple syrup.

Strawberry & Peanut Butter Crumble

If you've never tried strawberry crumble, you must. It's a summer staple at The Pudding Stop. This combination came from running out of custard one day and having only peanut butter ice cream to serve with it – it was impulsive, but emulated the All-American peanut butter and jelly combo. 'PB & J' was in the ration pack of US soldiers fuelling the troops during World War Two.

Serves 8

1kg strawberries, hulled

250g ground almonds

150g caster sugar

For the crumble topping

250g unsalted butter, chilled and diced

350g plain flour

100g demerara sugar

100g caster sugar

A pinch of sea salt

150g unsalted peanuts, lightly crushed

8 dollops of chunky peanut butter

Preheat the oven to 200°C/180°C fan/400°F/Gas mark 6.

Place the strawberries in a round 28 x 5cm ceramic dish and sprinkle with the ground almonds (to soak up excess liquid) and sugar.

For the crumble topping, use your fingertips to rub the butter into the flour, leaving some chunky clumps. Stir in both sugars, the salt and the nuts. Spread evenly over the strawberries.

Wet 2 teaspoons, then dot little spoonfuls of peanut butter at random intervals over the crumble – they will melt into the crumble as it bakes.

Bake for 30 minutes, until the crumble is golden brown and the rich red strawberries are bubbling through. Remove from the oven and leave to rest before serving with cream, or peanut butter ice cream if you can get your hands on it.

Gooseberry & Elderflower Suet Pudding

Gooseberries and elderflowers are in season at the same time and taste wonderful together – gooseberries bring a tartness and elderflower a floral flagrancy. Elderflower is bountiful in summer hedgerows and makes for easy foraging. No one appreciates the gooseberry like the English – perhaps because they suffer neither from English weather nor negligent gardening. My father-in-law is an excellent gardener and his gooseberry bushes yield over a hundred pounds of gooseberries every year – enough to supply a small pudding shop for a few months of the year! And they're even delivered topped and tailed!

Serves 6

1kg gooseberries, topped and tailed

500g caster sugar

200ml elderflower cordial (homemade if you have some)

1 batch of Suet Pastry (see page 24)

Firstly, prepare the gooseberry filling. Place the gooseberries and sugar in a saucepan over a medium heat and cook gently until the gooseberries are soft and squidgy. Remove from the heat and strain the fruit, reserving the cooking liquor in a separate pan.

Place the cooking liquor over a high heat, add the elderflower cordial and reduce to a sticky syrup. Remove from the heat and toss in the cooked gooseberries. Set aside and leave to cool completely.

Roll out the pastry on a floured work surface to 3mm thick to create a round at least twice the diameter of a 1-litre pudding basin. Cut away a quarter section from the pastry – set aside to use as the lid.

Use the larger section of pastry to line the bottom and sides of the pudding basin, tucking the pastry closely to the edge of the pudding basin and allowing it to overhang. Take the smaller piece of pastry and re-roll it to exactly fit the top of the pudding.

Fill the pudding with the gooseberries, place the pastry lid on top and seal well by pinching the pastry together where it meets. Trim off any excess with a knife.

Prepare the pudding for steaming (see page 13).

Place the pudding basin in a large saucepan with enough boiling water in the pan to come two-thirds of the way up the pudding. After 30–45 minutes, you may need to top up with boiling water. Steam for 2 hours until it is springy to touch.

When cooked, remove the pudding from the saucepan, release the string and parchment and invert onto a large plate. Serve warm with custard.

Apricot Tarte Tatin

When baking a tarte tatin, it's really important to select a fruit that will hold its shape and not melt into the caramel. Apples and pears work well – but I especially like apricots. You can also use shortcrust pastry in this recipe.

Serves 6–8

125g caster sugar, plus an extra handful

65g unsalted butter, plus an extra knob

10 apricots, halved and stoned

450g Quick Puff Pastry (see page 23)

Flour, for dusting

Preheat the oven to 200°C/180°C fan/400°F/Gas mark 6.

First, make the butterscotch. Put the sugar with 1 tablespoon of water in a 20–25cm ovenproof frying pan and cook over a high heat until the sugar turns to the colour of an old penny. Do not be tempted to stir the sugar, as it will crystallise. Do not take your eye off the caramel, as it will burn. Remove from the heat and whisk in the butter. Leave to rest for a few minutes.

When the butterscotch is smooth and silky, place the apricot cut side up in the butterscotch.

Roll out your pastry on a floured work surface to 3mm thick. Use a large plate to cut out a circle large enough to cover your frying pan, then lay the pastry over the apricots, tucking in any remaining pastry. Prick all over with a fork and dot with a knob of butter and a handful of caster sugar.

Bake for 30–35 minutes, or until golden brown. Remove the pan from the oven and leave to rest before inverting onto a large plate. Serve immediately with extra-thick cream or vanilla ice cream.

Apple & Bilberry Pie

Bilberries are native to the British Isles and are closely related to the North American blueberry. If you lived north of the Midlands a century ago you would almost certainly be eating bilberry pie every Sunday. Bilberries are tricky little berries to cultivate and so are usually found in the wild – enthusiastic foragers seek them in August and September. If you cannot find a bilberry bush, some supermarkets stock them in jars with syrup, or you can use blueberries.

Serves 8–10

250g Bramley apples, peeled, cored and sliced

250g Cox's Orange Pippins, peeled, cored and sliced

250g bilberries (drained of their syrup if using jarred) or blueberries

100g caster sugar, plus extra for sprinkling on top

1 batch of Shortcrust Pastry (see page 20), reserving a little to make stars (optional)

Flour, for dusting

1 egg, beaten

Preheat the oven to 200°C/180°C fan/400°F/Gas mark 6..

Put the apples in a round 28 x 5cm pie dish and stir in the bilberries. Arrange the fruit so that it mounds up in the middle. Sprinkle the fruit liberally with caster sugar as you are adding it so that the sugar is well dispersed. Pour cold water into the dish until it reaches halfway up the dish.

Roll out the pastry on a floured work surface to 3mm thick and cut a strip long enough to lie around the edge of the pie dish. Brush the rim of the pie dish with water, stick the strip of pastry to it, then brush with beaten egg.

Use the rest of the pastry to cover the pie dish and pinch to seal and crimp the edges to the rim using your thumb and first finger. Run a knife around the pie dish to neaten up any surplus pastry, using it to make some stars to go on top.

Make a hole in the middle of the pastry lid to allow steam to escape and insert a pie funnel if you have one to hand. Brush all over the pastry with the remaining beaten egg. Sprinkle liberally with caster sugar and bake for 15 minutes. Lower the oven temperature to 180°C/160°C fan/350°F/Gas mark 4. and bake for a further 45 minutes. Check the apples are cooked by inserting a sharp knife – if there is no resistance the pie is ready.

Remove from the oven and leave to rest before serving with custard.

Tip: Using a pie funnel will release any excess steam and will support the structure of the pie.

Apricot & Raspberry Crumble

This is another summer crumble. Fresh apricots are the fruit I look forward to most when they become available in early June. To make full use of the apricots, crack the stones and remove the kernels. They can be added to the crumble or used to flavour ice cream and custard.

Serves 8

100g butter

200g caster sugar

1 vanilla pod, split and seeds scraped out

600g apricots, halved and stoned

400g raspberries

For the crumble topping

350g plain flour

250g unsalted butter, chilled and diced

100g demerara sugar

100g caster sugar

A pinch of sea salt

75g hazelnuts, slightly crushed

75g flaked almonds

Preheat the oven to 180°C/160°C fan/350°F/Gas mark 4.

Put the butter, sugar and vanilla seeds in a heavy-based saucepan, and add the apricots. Cook for a few minutes over a medium to high heat, until it begins to caramelise. Remove from the heat and set aside while you make the crumble.

For the crumble topping, use your fingertips to rub the butter into the flour, leaving some chunky clumps. Stir in the sugars, the salt and the nuts. Add the apricolts and raspberries to a round 28 x 5cm pie dish and spread the crumble mix evenly over the fruit.

Bake for 30 minutes, until the crumble is golden brown and the fruits are bubbling through. Remove from the oven and leave to rest before serving with vanilla ice cream.

Baked Summer Pudding

To a summer pudding purist, what I am suggesting is sacreligious. Here I mix berries, I use brioche and worst of all I bake it – essentially rendering the pudding a Charlotte. I am a huge fan of a proper summer pudding and if you are too, then simply follow this recipe and leave it unbaked in the fridge overnight before serving, resulting in a more traditional version. You can use homemade bread instead of brioche but the cheap supermarket kind should be avoided as it gives a slimy texture.

Serves 6–8

1kg mixed summer berries (red-, white- or blackcurrants, strawberries, raspberries, blueberries)

400g caster sugar

1 brioche loaf (about 1kg)

Pile the berries into a saucepan over a medium heat and add 300g of sugar.

Cook the berries slowly until they have released all their lovely juices and have softened slightly. Have a final taste before you remove from the heat, and add the remaining 100g of sugar. When you're happy, set aside to cool.

Cut the crusts off the brioche and slice into thumb-width slices. Cut two circles from the loaf – one for the bottom of a 1-litre pudding basin, and one for the top. Cut the remaining slices in half to form triangles.

Strain the fruit through a fine sieve, catching the juices in a bowl, and place the berries in another bowl. You are now ready to assemble the pudding.

Dip both sides of the smallest circle in the fruit juice and place on the bottom of a 1-litre pudding basin. Line the sides of the basin with the triangle pieces, dipping in the juice and overlapping them, plugging any gaps, as you go.

When you're happy that the dish is fully lined and sealed, pour in the berries until they just come to the top of the basin, leaving some space for the lid. Dip the lid in the juice and place on top. Place a circle of baking parchment on top, then an ovenproof plate and a 1kg weight. Place in the fridge overnight.

The next day: At this point you can eat it cold with cream but if you would like to bake it, preheat the oven to 190°C/170°C fan/375°F/Gas mark 5. Bake the pudding for 30 minutes with the plate and weight still in place. Remove from the oven, remove the plate and weight and bake for a further 10 minutes, or until golden and crispy on top. Leave to rest for 10 minutes, then invert the pudding, turn out onto a large plate, decorate with berries and serve with cream.

Cherry Pie

The cherry season in Kent runs from mid-June to early in August. They are the finest of the English summer fruits. Picked and eaten fresh from a wooden crate, they need no cooking. They're tasty enough to put on our shop menu as a 'bowl of Kent cherries'. However, for when the English summer turns sour, there's no finer pudding than a warm cherry pie.

Serves 8–10

200g cherry jam (or any red berry jam)

2 tablespoons cornflour

150ml boiling water

1kg Kentish cherries, stalks and stones removed

500g Shortcrust Pastry (see page 20)

Flour, for dusting

1 large egg, beaten

Caster sugar, for sprinkling

Preheat the oven to 200°C/180°C fan/400°F/Gas mark 6. Butter a round 28 x 5cm round pie dish.

Place the jam in a saucepan over a medium heat, and whisk in the cornflour. Slowly pour in the boiling water, whisking continuously, until you have a silky and smooth sauce. Simmer for a few moments, until it thickens slightly and coats the back of a tablespoon. Remove from the heat and stir in the cherries so that they are all well coated.

Roll out two-thirds of the pastry on a floured work surface to 3mm thick, and use it to line the buttered pie dish. Prick all over with a fork and bake blind in the oven for 15–20 minutes, or until golden brown. Remove from the oven and brush liberally with the beaten egg. Return the pie case to the oven for 1 minute or until the egg wash has dried.

Pour in the cherry mixture, encouraging the cherries to form a mound in the middle. Roll out the remaining pastry and use it to cover the pie. Seal and crimp the edges using your thumb and first finger, and run a knife around the pie dish to neaten up any surplus pastry.

Brush all over with the remaining beaten egg and sprinkle liberally with caster sugar. Reduce the oven temperature to 180°C/160°C fan/350°F/Gas mark 4 and bake the pie for 30–35 minutes. Remove from the oven and leave to rest before serving with extra-thick cream.

Lemon Tart (& Lemon Meringue Pie)

It is vital that you make this tart the day you are eating it and not in advance, otherwise the pastry will become soggy and the lemon filling will crack. The perfect lemon tart has pastry with bite to contrast with the silky, tangy, lemony, vibrant filling. To turn it from a tart to a pie, follow the steps below.

Serves 8–10

1 batch of Sweet Pastry (see page 21)

Flour, for dusting

3 eggs, plus an extra one, beaten

300ml double cream

270g caster sugar

6 egg yolks (whites reserved for the meringue)

Grated zest and juice of 3 lemons

For the meringue pie (optional)

6 egg whites (from the separated eggs above)

Caster sugar (exactly double the weight of the egg whites)

3 teaspoons cornflour

Preheat the oven to 180°C/160°C fan/350°F/Gas mark 4 . Roll out the pastry on a floured work surface to 3mm thick, and use it to line a greased 23cm loose-bottomed fluted tart tin. Prick the base all over with a fork, and chill for 30 minutes. Line the pastry shell with foil and baking beans, then bake blind for 15 minutes. Remove from the oven and take the foil and baking beans away. Bake for another 5 minutes, until the pastry is golden brown. Brush the pastry with the beaten egg and return to the oven for 1–2 minutes, until it is a good golden brown colour all over, then set aside. Reduce the oven temperature to 110°C/90°C fan/225°F/Gas mark ¼.

Put the cream in a saucepan over a moderate heat, and heat until just below boiling point. Meanwhile, whisk the caster sugar, whole eggs and egg yolks together in a bowl, then pour over the hot cream, whisking continuously. Stir in the lemon juice, strain into a jug, then stir in the lemon zest. Leave to rest for 10 minutes, then skim off and discard any foam with a spoon. Place the pastry case on the oven shelf and carefully pour the lemon filling inside. Bake for 45–55 minutes, or until a slight quiver remains on the surface of the tart. Remove from the oven and leave to cool before serving with cream.

To turn it into a Lemon Meringue Pie, increase the oven temperature to 170°C/150°C fan/335°F/Gas mark 3. Weigh the leftover egg whites and measure out exactly double this weight of caster sugar. Whisk the whites until they form soft peaks. Add all the sugar and whisk continuously until you have stiff, glossy peaks. To test it's ready, rub the meringue between your thumb and first finger to ensure it doesn't feel grainy. Stir in the cornflour.

Pile this meringue on top of the tart, arranging it in a large mountain shape, and make peaks by swirling with a spoon. Bake for 15–20 minutes, until the meringue is lightly golden and crisp. Serve warm or cold.

Spiced Nectarine Tart

Serves 8–10

Nectarines have smooth skins and peaches have velvety ones, and both are beautiful fruits to eat. This is a baked tart, and nectarines fare particularly well when baked – softening without losing their integrity, especially when paired with a few warming spices.

For the tart

1 batch of Almond Pastry (see page 22)

Flour, for dusting

Butter, for greasing

1 egg, beaten

8–10 nectarines, stoned, cut into a mixture of halves and quarters

For the topping

300g unsalted butter, softened

300g light brown soft sugar

3 egg yolks

Grated zest of 1 lemon

300g plain flour

60g spelt flour

40g rolled oats

A pinch of salt

1½ teaspoons baking powder

2 teaspoons freshly ground black peppercorns

2 teaspoons ground allspice

2 teaspoons ground star anise

Extra demerara sugar, for sprinkling

The day before you want to make this tart:

Beat the butter, sugar, egg yolks, lemon zest, flours, oats, salt, baking powder and the ground spices until you have a smooth dough. Turn out onto a work surface and knead into a smooth ball. Wrap in cling film and place in the freezer overnight.

The next day:

Preheat the oven to 180°C/160°C fan/350°F/Gas mark 4.

Roll out the pastry on a floured work surface to 3mm thick, and large enough to line a 30cm tart tin. Brush the tin with butter, line with the pastry and prick it all over with a fork.

Line the pastry shell with foil and fill with baking beans. Bake for about 15 minutes, until golden brown around the edges. Remove the foil and baking beans and return the pastry case to the oven for 1–2 minutes, until it is a good golden brown colour all over. Remove from the oven, brush with the beaten egg and return to the oven for 1–2 minutes until golden brown. Set aside. Reduce the oven temperature to 160°C/140°C fan/320°F/Gas mark 2.

Arrange the nectarine halves and quarters inside the tart shell, squashing them down if necessary. Take your dough from the freezer and grate it on top of the nectarines. The dough will melt and move through the tart, so don't be afraid to use it all. Spread it out with your hands, filling in any gaps. Bake for 50 minutes.

With 15 minutes to go, remove the tart from the oven, squish down the nectarines and pastry with the back of a spoon and smooth the top of the tart. Return to the oven, until the juices from the nectarines are bubbling over. Remove from the oven and leave to cool slightly before serving with ice cream.

Rhubarb Charlotte

A Charlotte is a pudding that is either baked using seasonal fruit and encased within sliced bread, or unbaked using sponge fingers, fruit and bavarois – much like a trifle. This recipe is for a baked Charlotte. Apple Charlotte is the most traditional form, but this pudding calls for custard – and custard in turn calls for rhubarb.

Serves 6

A large knob of butter, plus a little extra melted butter for brushing

1 vanilla pod, split and seeds scraped out

1 large Bramley apple, peeled, cored and diced

350g forced Yorkshire rhubarb, chopped into 2cm batons

250g caster sugar

1 crusty white bread loaf or brioche (about 1kg)

Put a saucepan over a medium heat and add the knob of butter, vanilla seeds and diced apple. Cook slowly until the apple is soft but with a little bite. Add the rhubarb and sugar and cook for a little longer, until the rhubarb and apple have softened. Strain to remove any excess liquid into a saucepan. You can reduce this and add it back to the fruit if necessary.

Cut the crusts off your loaf and slice into thumb-width slices. Work out how much bread you will need to line a 1-litre pudding basin. If you have a circular pastry cutter, cut out circles for the top and bottom to make it easy for you. Liberally brush the slices of bread (and circles) on both sides with melted butter and use them to line a greased pudding basin, putting the bottom circle in first and then filling around the sides. Overlap the bread to avoid any gaps and pack the slices in tightly.

When you have completed the sides and bottom, fill with the rhubarb and apple, leaving enough space for the circular bread lid on top. Top with the bread lid, on top of which place a circle of parchment paper cut to size. Place an ovenproof plate on top of the pudding along with a 1kg weight. Put the weighted pudding in the fridge for an hour or so.

Preheat the oven to 200°C/180°C fan/400°F/Gas mark 6. Bake the Charlotte with the plate and weight in place for 30 minutes. Remove from the oven, remove the plate and weight and then bake for a further 10 minutes, until the pudding is golden brown. Remove from the oven again and leave to rest for a moment before inverting onto a warmed plate and serving with custard.

Buttermilk Pancakes

We serve these pancakes in The Pudding Stop for brunch every morning as an antidote to our relentless world of serving one sticky toffee pudding after another. They are great served with blueberry compote, crisp bacon and maple syrup, or with seasonal stewed fruit, yoghurt and honey. There's no reason they couldn't be eaten at any time of the day, especially after supper, with the traditional squeeze of lemon juice and a liberal sprinkling of sugar.

Makes about 20 small American-style pancakes

550g plain flour (buckwheat, rye or spelt also work well, adding delicious flavour)

60g caster sugar

4 teaspoons baking powder

2 teaspoons bicarbonate of soda

½ teaspoon sea salt flakes

525ml buttermilk, well shaken

525ml natural yoghurt

4 large eggs

125ml sunflower oil

Clarified butter (see page 42), for frying

Greek yoghurt, fruit compote and honey, to serve

Measure and mix all the dry ingredients, excluding the salt, in a bowl. Pass it all through a sieve into a bowl, then add the salt. Combine the wet ingredients in another bowl and lightly whisk.

Add the wet ingredients to the dry ingredients and whisk until ONLY just combined.

Preheat a saucepan over a moderate heat for 10 minutes prior to frying the first pancake.

Place a teaspoon of clarified butter in the pan, melt then wipe off with kitchen paper. Place one level ¼ cup measure of pancake mixture per pancake in the hot pan and cook for 2–3 minutes, or until bubbles appear on the surface of the pancake.

Carefully flip the pancake and cook for a further 1–2 minutes on the other side.

Serve with fruit compote, yoghurt and honey, or vanilla ice cream and chocolate sauce.

Tip: If you don't want to make this many pancakes in one go, the batter will keep well in the fridge for a couple of days.

Refreshing

Stewed & Poached Fruits

Strawberry Daiquiri Mousse

Lemon Posset

Poached Poire Williams

Rhubarb & Cardamom Fool

Blackcurrant Fool

Banoffee Bocker Glory

Raspberry Pavlova

Blood Orange Jelly

Rocky Road Sundae

Strawberry & Rhubarb Jelly

Peach Melba

With the exceptions of my Rhubarb & Cardamom Fool and Raspberry Pavlova, the common theme of this chapter is that each pudding absolves you of the need for an oven. Very sensible at the height of summer when you crave the cool sensation of a scoop of ice cream or a chilled posset on your tongue. Pavlova is such a lovely summery pudding. Served chilled, the only effort comes from leaving it to bake in the oven, which you can do last thing at night when the air is cooler, leaving it in the oven to cool overnight until the next day.

The chapter starts with my favourite recipes for poached and stewed seasonal fruits, which also complement many of the puddings in other chapters. Cooked fruits are a wonderful and versatile accompaniment to many puddings. They can be served warm with ice cream or cold with a custard tart. Not only are they delicious and super-easy, they are a handy addition to your arsenal when you want a simple pudding or need to jazz up a pud. Stew a large batch and leave in the fridge or freezer so you can go back to them again and again as required.

This chapter also contains jellies, mousses, sundaes and fools – all of which are really refreshing and of course synonymous with summer. It is well known at The Pudding Stop that I am a huge jelly fan. Jelly and ice cream with perhaps a little shortbread on the side is something I could eat any day and at any time. As I mention later on in this chapter, jelly has been a victim of the food industry's scaling up and pricing down, so it has lost favour in recent times. However, the jelly I love and the jelly that I persuade my pudding punters to prioritise ahead of crumble and brownies when picking their pudding, is a fragrant, fruity, wobbly and silky-textured jelly. Jelly that should be celebrated by us now as Victorians did more than 100 years ago.

My fools and sundaes are more assembly jobs than recipes. As long as you have ice cream in the freezer and a selection of my sauces or stewed fruits ready to go, you will be able to whip them up instantly as an impromptu end to your meal.

Mr Pud's Poached Plums

Poached plums with star anise and vanilla are my favourite. They can be used to make a quick crumble, or served on Poor Knights of Windsor (see page 42) or Buttermilk Pancakes (see page 128) with yoghurt and honey.

(see page 42) or Buttermilk Pancakes (see page 128)

Makes about 10 portions

1kg plums, stoned

200g caster sugar

300ml cold water

1 vanilla pod, split and seeds scraped out

2 whole star anise

You can cook the plums in halves or sliced into segments – the bigger the pieces, the longer they will take to cook, but you will have better control over the cooking and a more consistent texture.

Put all the ingredients in a saucepan and cook over the lowest heat possible, until the plums are soft and tender and their juices have been released.

Strain the plums through a sieve and reserve the poaching liquid in a separate saucepan. Place this saucepan on the heat and reduce to a thick sauce that sticks to the back of a spoon.

Remove from the heat and leave to cool for a while before adding the plums back to the reduced liquid. The plums will keep for 3–4 days in the fridge or up to a month in the freezer.

Poached Yorkshire Rhubarb

You could serve this rhubarb with a custard tart, a slice of cheesecake or a buttermilk pudding, or simply serve it warm with a bowl of custard.

Makes about 10 portions

1kg forced Yorkshire rhubarb, cut into 2cm batons

300g caster sugar

300ml cold water

1 vanilla pod, split and seeds scraped out

Put all the ingredients in a saucepan and cook over the lowest heat possible, until the rhubarb is soft and tender and its juices have been released.

Strain the rhubarb through a sieve and reserve the poaching liquid in a separate saucepan. Place this saucepan on the heat and reduce to a thick sauce that sticks to the back of a spoon.

Remove from the heat and leave to cool for a while before adding the cooked rhubarb. The rhubarb will keep for 3–4 days in the fridge or a month in the freezer.

Stewed Bramley Apples

This can form the base of a quick crumble or can be chilled and saved for my dairy-free Bramley Apple Upside Down Pudding (see page 74) or Everlasting Apple Cidre Syllabub (see page 96).

Makes about 8 portions

625g Bramley apples, peeled, cored and diced

50g caster sugar

50ml water

4 cinnamon sticks

1 vanilla pod, split and seeds scraped out

Put all the ingredients in a saucepan and cook over the lowest heat possible, until the apple pieces are soft and tender. Remove from the heat and set aside.

If you think there is too much moisture, place the apples in a sieve and allow any excess liquid to drip through into a clean pan. This liquid can then be boiled and reduced to a sticky syrup and stirred back into the apples.

The apples can either be chilled for another day to use as a base for a crumble, or served warm. They will keep for 3–4 days in the fridge or a month in the freezer.

Strawberry Daiquiri Mousse

The daiquiri is thought to be an export from Cuba, and became popular in the 1940s when US president Franklin D. Roosevelt improved trade relations with Latin America, Cuba and the Caribbean, hence freeing up the import of rum. Rum, lime and sugar are the main ingredients in a daiquiri – and the strawberry daiquiri is the most well-known version. This strawberry mousse has all the flavours of a daiquiri and all the refreshment of a summer mousse.

Serves 6

450g strawberries, hulled

10g bronze leaf gelatine

1 tablespoon cornflour

2 egg yolks

75g caster sugar

150ml full-fat milk

4 tablespoons white rum

Grated zest and juice of 1 lime

300ml double cream

Put the strawberries in a food processor or blender and blitz to a purée. Pass the purée through a sieve into a bowl. Soak the gelatine in a bowl of water for 1–2 minutes, until soft.

Whisk the cornflour, egg yolks, sugar and a splash of milk together in a bowl. Put the remaining milk in a saucepan and bring to the boil over a medium heat. Slowly pour the hot milk over the egg mixture, whisking continuously. When fully combined, return the whisked mixture to the pan and cook over a medium heat until you have a thick custard.

Drain the gelatine, squeezing out any excess water, and whisk it into the custard along with the rum, lime and strawberry purée. Leave the custard to cool, with a layer of cling film on top to prevent a skin forming.

Whip the cream to soft peaks, then fold it into the cool fruity custard. Pour into individual glasses or bowls and leave to chill for several hours or overnight. This can be stored in the fridge and is best eaten within 1–2 days.

Lemon Posset

'And with sudden vigour it doth posset, And curd, like sour droppings into milk, The thin and wholesome blood.' William Shakespeare, Hamlet

A posset of the sixteenth and seventeenth centuries barely resembles the posset of today. Back then, a posset's make-up was curdled milk, enriched with sugar and alcohol, served warm in teapots to allow the liquid to be drunk and the curds to settle. They were thought to have medicinal benefits, curing common colds and fevers. I urge you to prove this theory and enjoy this posset while you're at it.

Makes 4

450ml double cream

150g caster sugar

1 vanilla pod, split and seeds scraped out

Grated zest and juice of 2 lemons

Raspberries and shortbread, to serve

Put the cream, sugar and vanilla pod and seeds into a saucepan and bring to the boil over a medium heat. Boil for 2–3 minutes, then set aside to cool.

Add the lemon zest and juice and stir through. Pour into four ramekins or small glasses and place in the fridge to set for several hours or overnight.

Serve with some fresh raspberries and shortbread. This can be stored in the fridge and is best eaten within 3 days.

Poached Poire William

Poire William is a French pear brandy made using the Williams pear. Some distillers attach bottles to budding trees so a whole pear grows inside. What better way to poach a pear than in boozy liquid pear?

Serves 6

1.5 litres cold water

250g caster sugar

1 vanilla pod, split and seeds scraped out

1 star anise

1 bay leaf

6 whole Conference pears, peeled and stalks left intact (cut off the bottom of each pear so it stands up)

6 tablespoons Poire William, added to taste

Put the water, sugar, vanilla pod and seeds, star anise and bay leaf in a saucepan and bring to a rolling simmer. Submerge each pear in the liquor, standing them up and packing them neatly together. Cook for 10–15 minutes, or until inserting a sharp knife offers little resistance. Baste the pears regularly with the poaching syrup.

Remove the pears with a slotted spoon and turn up the heat to reduce the liquor to a sticky syrup. Remove from the heat and leave to cool slightly before adding Poire William to your taste.

To serve, place a pear in a bowl, pour over some of the cooking syrup and add a scoop of almost-melting vanilla ice cream. The pears can be kept in the fridge and are best eaten within 1–2 days.

Tip: You could use any other brandy such as Armagnac if you prefer.

Rhubarb & Cardamom Fool

This fool has the dream combination of rhubarb, cardamom, custard and cream. Rhubarb is roasted with the cardamom to intensify the flavour, while cardamom complements rhubarb very well. Cardamom goes similarly well in creamy puddings, which is why it works here alongside the custard and lightly whipped cream.

Serves 4–6

500g rhubarb, cut into 5cm batons

10 cardamom pods, cracked

300ml chilled Custard (see page 216)

300ml double cream

175g caster sugar

Preheat the oven to 160°C/140°C fan/320°F/Gas mark 2 and line a baking tray with baking parchment.

Put the rhubarb and cardamom on the baking tray and sprinkle over 75g of the sugar. Bake for 15–20 minutes, or until the rhubarb is soft and tender. Remove from the oven and carefully pour any excess liquid through a sieve into a saucepan. Discard the cardamom pods.

Place the saucepan on the stove over a high heat and boil to reduce to a thick syrup. Remove from the heat and stir in the cooked rhubarb and the remaining sugar. Place in the fridge until fully chilled.

When ready to serve, remove the custard and rhubarb from the fridge and combine in a bowl. Whip the cream to soft peaks and carefully fold it into the rhubarb and custard to create a rippled effect. Serve in bowls with a piece of shortbread. Best eaten immediately, or can be left overnight.

Blackcurrant Fool

Blackcurrants are the most trusting of fruits and they make the best fools. The colour of the cream changes to a pinky-purple as the blackcurrants burst, creating a very pretty pudding.

Serves 4–6

500g blackcurrants

About 200g caster sugar, plus extra if required

150ml single cream

150ml double cream

Put the blackcurrants and a handful of the sugar in a saucepan over a moderate heat. Cook for 5 minutes or so, until the juices are released. Taste and add more sugar if necessary, but be careful not to make the fool too sweet. Leave to cool in the fridge.

Whip both creams together in a bowl, then fold it into the cooled fruits. Serve lightly chilled. Best eaten immediately, or can be left overnight.

Tip: It's perfectly fine to use all double cream or all single depending on how rich you'd like it to taste.

Banoffee Bocker Glory

The Knickerbocker Glory appears to be an American invention, with knickerbockers being trousers worn by Dutch settlers in seventeenth century New York. Centuries later the New York basketball team was nicknamed the Knicks. Perhaps this ice cream sundae, layered with fruit, jelly, chocolate sauce, whipped cream, ice cream and a cherry was made every time the Knicks were victorious! My version incorporates all those favourite flavours associated with a banoffee pie: banana, toffee, chocolate and cream. Next time you find glory, invent one – and name it after yourself.

Serves 1

1 chocolate digestive, bashed up

1 ripe banana, peeled and sliced

2 tablespoons Salted Caramel Chocolate Sauce (see page 215)

2 tablespoons Butterscotch Sauce (see page 213)

2 scoops of ice cream (vanilla, chocolate or banana all work well)

50ml double cream, lightly whipped

4–5 pecan nuts, lightly toasted

Put the bashed-up chocolate digestive into the bottom of a tall sundae glass.

Place a scoop of ice cream on top, then the butterscotch sauce, followed by half of the banana pieces.

Add a scoop of ice cream, the Salted Caramel Chocolate Sauce and the remaining banana. Top with some whipped cream and finish with the pecans.

Tip: This is more of an assembly job than a recipe, and relies on you having all the component parts ready to go.

Raspberry Pavlova

Anna Pavlova was the Russian ballerina most famous for playing the role of 'The Dying Swan' and was the first to take her ballet tour around the world. And so it was on tour that a chef in Wellington created a tasty dessert with meringue, whipped cream and fruit, and named it after her. The key to a good pavlova is the addition of cornflour and white wine vinegar to create a chewy marshmallowy centre.

Serves 8

4 egg whites (weigh them)

320g caster sugar – or exactly double the weight of the egg whites

2 teaspoons cornflour

2 teaspoons white wine vinegar

1 batch of Vanilla Cream (see page 223), to serve

For the raspberries

600g raspberries

3 tablespoons caster sugar

2 teaspoons lemon juice

Preheat the oven to 150°C/130°C fan/300°F/Gas mark 2.

Whisk the egg whites in a very clean bowl, until soft peaks form. Turn off the mixer and add all the sugar. Whisk on high until the meringue is thick, glossy and no grains are left when you rub a little of the meringue between your first finger and thumb. Finally, whisk in the cornflour and white wine vinegar.

Pile the mixture onto a baking sheet so that the meringue is perfectly round and at least 5cm high. Bake for 1 hour, until the meringue has risen and is firm to touch. Turn off the oven and leave in the oven to cool completely, with the door slightly ajar.

Meanwhile, put 350g of the raspberries, the sugar and the lemon juice in a saucepan over a medium heat and cook for 5–10 minutes, until soft and dark red. Pass through a sieve and leave to cool.

To assemble the pavlova, place the meringue on a large plate and spread the Vanilla Cream over the top, forming a mound in the middle. Carefully place the remaining uncooked raspberries on top and pour over the cooled raspberry sauce. Serve immediately.

Blood Orange Jelly

Everyone knows the Victorians liked to show off – and a feast was just the occasion to do it. Elaborate jellies would form the centrepiece of the table and would be the crowning glory of the feast. Jelly perfectly conveyed the advance of the Industrial Revolution in Britain – with the availability of cheap factory-made gelatine and copper jelly moulds. In January, I find the blood orange season and the prospect of this jelly is surprisingly welcome after the festive frivolities.

Serves 4

700ml blood orange juice, or about 9 juiced blood oranges

4 tablespoons caster sugar, or more or less to taste

10–15g bronze leaf gelatine (about 4 sheets)

Pass the juice through a sieve into a small saucepan set on some digital scales. Add the caster sugar, 1 tablespoon at a time, until it is the right sweetness for you. Write down the total weight of this mixture.

Place the saucepan over a low heat and gently warm to dissolve the sugar. Do not boil.

For the perfect jelly wobble, you need to work with a ratio of 565ml of liquid to 10g of gelatine. Place the gelatine in a bowl of cold water (it must be cold to not interfere with the setting process later) and, when soft, squeeze out any excess water. Whisk the gelatine into the warm orange juice until completely dissolved and pass through a jelly bag into a jug.

Pour the mixture into a jelly mould and leave to set in the fridge for several hours.

To serve, submerge the mould in a bowl of warm water until the jelly begins to come away from the sides. Remove from the water and invert the jelly onto a plate. Holding onto both the mould and plate, give them a shake and carefully lift away the mould. Serve with blood orange segments, vanilla cream and shortbread.

Tip: Bronze leaf gelatine is better quality than powdered gelatine and ensures a consistent set. Each sheet measures 23 x 7cm and weighs about 3g.

Rocky Road Sundae

At the peak of the summer, with a beautiful bounty of British berries bursting onto our menu – in the form of steamed sponges, jellies, fools, mousses, pavlovas, crumbles and pies – I am always disheartened to find that my Rocky Road Sundae is the number one seller. It does taste delicious, but frankly it's vulgar and you should be ashamed to make it, as I am ashamed to share it with you. Oh well – like I said – it is delicious.

Makes 1 sundae

A piece of Rocky Road (see page 178)

1 scoop of vanilla ice cream

2 tablespoons Butterscotch Sauce (see page 213)

1 scoop of salted caramel or chocolate ice cream

2 tablespoons Salted Caramel Chocolate Sauce (see page 215)

To assemble, cut the square of rocky road into 16 small cubes. Place a third of them in the bottom of a tall sundae dish.

Place a scoop of ice cream on top, followed by the butterscotch sauce.

Repeat with another third of the rocky road pieces and a different ice cream. Top with the last of the rocky road and the chocolate sauce.

Strawberry & Rhubarb Jelly

Jelly was a major victim of commercialisation, so no wonder it has lost favour recently – but this will remind you how good jelly can be, and what a wonderful combination strawberry and rhubarb is. The general rule is 565ml of liquid to 10g of gelatine to achieve the perfect wobble. And, achieving the perfect wobble is as much fun as eating the jelly.

Makes 6 jellies

400g strawberries

400g rhubarb

1 vanilla pod, split and seeds scraped out

200g caster sugar, or more or less to taste

About 20g bronze leaf gelatine (about 6 sheets)

Put the strawberries, rhubarb, vanilla pod and seeds and sugar in a saucepan with 1 tablespoon cold water and cook over a medium heat with the lid on for about 20 minutes, until the fruit is soft and mushy with lots of juice in the pan.

Strain the liquid through a sieve into a clean pan (or for a crystal-clear jelly, strain through a jelly bag). Weigh the juice and calculate how much gelatine you need (see above).

Place the gelatine in a bowl of cold water to soften. Meanwhile, put the fruit juice back over the heat and gently warm to blood temperature. Squeeze the excess water from the gelatine, then whisk it into the warm juice until fully dissolved.

Pass through a sieve into a jug. Disperse between six 175ml moulds and transfer to the fridge for several hours to set.

Serve with soft-scoop vanilla ice cream.

Peach Melba

This was created in the early 1890s at the Savoy Hotel in London for Nellie Melba, the Australian operatic soprano, by legendary French chef Georges Auguste Escoffier – a master of making the elaborate simple. This timeless combination of peaches, vanilla ice cream and raspberries is simply unsurpassable perfection.

Serves 6

A knob of butter

6 perfectly ripe peaches, stoned and halved

A squirt of runny honey

6 scoops vanilla ice cream

For the raspberry sauce

350g raspberries

3 tablespoons caster sugar

2 teaspoons lemon juice

First, make the raspberry sauce. Put the raspberries, sugar and lemon juice in a saucepan over a medium heat and cook for 5–10 minutes, until soft and dark red. Pass through a sieve and leave to cool.

Place a frying pan over a medium heat and add the butter and 1 tablespoon water. When it is foaming, add the peach halves, flat side down, and squirt some runny honey on top. Cook for 3–4 minutes, before turning onto the other side. Turn the heat down slightly and cook for a further 5 minutes until soft and tender.

Transfer the peach halves to a warm plate, and add a scoop of vanilla ice cream and a generous drizzle of raspberry sauce to finish.

Chocolate

———◆———

Brownies

Little Chocolate Pots

Steamed Banana Choc Chip Sponge

Flourless Chocolate Cake

Steamed Chocolate Pudding

Baked Chocolate Tart

Salted Caramel & Peanut Butter
Chocolate Brownies

Chocolate Madeleines

Rocky Road

Chocolate Mousse

Chocolate, like tea and coffee, is processed from a natural commodity that has been traded for hundreds of years – yet many modern chocolate products resemble little of the pure cacao that was first made into a drink by South American Aztecs and Mayans. The seeds of the Theobroma cacao 'chocolate tree' (chocolate DOES grow on trees) must be fermented, dried, cleaned and then roasted to develop flavour. Once roasted, the shells are discarded to leave the cacao nibs, which are ground to produce 100 per cent cacao mass – the purest form of chocolate. This mass can then be processed into two further components: cocoa butter and cocoa solids.

The more cocoa solids, the darker the chocolate will be. Quality dark chocolate will typically contain at least 70 per cent cocoa solids, milk chocolate up to 50 per cent, and white chocolate has no cocoa solids but contains a maximum of 35 per cent cocoa butter mixed with ingredients such as fat, sugar and milk. It is these three ingredients that sweeten and alter the flavour of chocolate. The reason dark chocolate, along with red wine, is often stated to have health benefits is linked to it containing high amounts of antioxidants. And like wine and coffee, chocolate's flavour varies greatly depending on where it has been grown. Half of all chocolate is produced in the Ivory Coast, and is the Forastero variety. These are the easiest cacao trees to cultivate, as they are hardy and high yielding. They produce chocolate with a typical taste that is brief on the palate and offers no secondary flavours – perfect for use in cheap mainstream confectionery where other flavours will be added. Consider this similar to the Robusta coffee bean – used to produce the cheapest coffee.

The most prized cacao pods that produce the most expensive chocolate are the Criollo, native to South America and the Carribean. Criollo crops produce chocolate with little of the everyday chocolate taste, but rich in secondary citrus, caramel and nutty notes. It is this chocolate that I urge you to invest in when baking at home – you will be rewarded with chocolate brownies, mousses, cakes, puddings and tarts with a far superior chocolate flavour to those bought in your local store, and even perhaps your local café.

Brownies

The brownie is a modern-day phenomenon – everyone likes it a certain way and claims to have THE perfect recipe. You can use milk chocolate or dark chocolate, cocoa powder, nuts or no nuts, vanilla and spices, dried fruit; even add your favourite chocolate bar. The MOST important thing is that you do not over-bake brownies. This is a recipe that allows you to create different flavours and offers a few alternatives for different people and different occasions – you can substitute the flour for rice flour to make the brownies gluten-free, for example. Perfect for a lunchbox, or a pick-me-up on an afternoon stroll.

Makes 15

375g butter

300g of the best dark chocolate you can afford, broken or chopped into small pieces

6 large eggs, lightly beaten

300g caster sugar

200g dark brown muscovado sugar

120g plain or rice flour (we often use brown rice flour for extra flavour)

80g cocoa powder

1 teaspoon flaked sea salt

Preheat the oven to 180°C/160°C fan/350°F/Gas mark 4 and line a 35 x 25 x 5cm baking tin with baking parchment.

Melt the butter in a saucepan over a medium heat and stir in the chocolate.

Whisk the eggs with the sugars in a bowl, then add them to the chocolate mix.

Sift the flour and cocoa powder into the pan and stir in the salt.

Pour the mixture into the baking tin and bake for 20 minutes.

Remove from the oven and leave to cool, or leave for 10–15 minutes before serving warm with vanilla ice cream and Salted Caramel Chocolate Sauce (see page 215).

Tip: These are a few credible combinations to try, which can be added to the batter before pouring into the baking tin:

- *Dried fruits and nuts – add 35g of each variety*

- *Shelled hazelnuts and almonds – add 35g of each*

- *Pedro-Pimped Prunes (see page 226) – add 50g prunes and 2 tablespoons of the liquor*

Little Chocolate Pots

These little chocolate pots are absolutely delicious – they're ridiculously easy to make and create an amazing silky smooth texture that falls somewhere in between a mousse and a ganache. You can keep them plain or experiment by infusing the milk with a sprig of rosemary, star anise, a vanilla pod or orange zest. There's no egg in these pots, so they're good to keep for a few days and are ideal for those who can't eat egg.

Makes 8 little pots, or 4 big ones!

360ml full-fat milk

420g of the best dark chocolate you can afford (minimum 70% cocoa solids)

360g condensed milk

60g unsalted butter

A pinch of sea salt

A bar of milk or dark chocolate

Optional extras

Fresh rosemary sprig

Star anise

Vanilla pod

Grated orange zest

If you would like to add a certain flavour to the chocolate pot, place your optional extra with the milk in a saucepan over a moderate heat and bring to the boil. Remove from the heat and leave to infuse for a few hours. Remember to remove your chosen extra ingredient before you start making the little chocolate pots, by straining the milk.

Warm the milk (infused or plain), chocolate, condensed milk, butter and a pinch of salt together in a large saucepan over a medium to low heat, stirring occasionally, to encourage the melting process. When the chocolate and butter have fully melted, increase the heat and whisk the mixture until it is glossy and smooth.

Divide the mixture between ramekins or glasses, and place in the fridge for several hours or overnight to cool.

When ready to serve, take the bar of chocolate and use a sharp kitchen knife to scrape shards of chocolate from the bar (or you could use a grater). Scatter liberally over each decadent little chocolate pot. Serve with Chocolate Madeleines (see page 176) hot from the oven.

Steamed Banana Choc Chip Sponge

Banana cake and custard have been served up as school dinners for decades. I fondly remember eating mine out of a little plastic bowl – essential sustenance for young lads forced to wear short trousers all year round. The addition of chocolate chips and chocolate custard really works with the sweet, sticky banana – it's perfect to make in the middle of winter for the young or the old, short or long trousers.

Serves 6

200g unsalted butter

200g light brown soft sugar

A pinch of sea salt

4 large eggs

400g self-raising flour

2 large, very ripe bananas, mashed

150g milk or dark chocolate chips

Cream the butter and sugar with the salt in the bowl of a stand mixer until pale and fluffy. Beat in the eggs one at a time with a handful of flour to prevent the mixture from curdling. Fold in the rest of the flour, then the mashed bananas and chocolate chips. Pour into a 1-litre pudding basin.

Prepare the pudding for steaming (see page 13). Place a large saucepan over a high heat, put the pudding inside and fill the pan halfway to two-thirds up the pudding basin with freshly boiled water. Quickly put a lid on and leave to boil for 1 hour and 30 minutes. Keep the water topped up with more boiling water if necessary. The pudding is done when it has risen fully and the sponge is springy to touch.

When cooked, remove the pudding from the saucepan, release the string and parchment and invert onto a large plate. Serve warm with Chocolate Custard (see page 217).

Flourless Chocolate Cake

This cake is just so chocolatey and gooey that you will find yourself making it over and over again. And, once baked, you will find yourself going back for another slice. It is perfect served cold with a dollop of tangy crème fraîche and a cup of coffee, or served warm as a pudding with chocolate sauce and a scoop of vanilla ice cream. It is important to under-cook the cake, much as you would with brownies, to ensure that the middle remains gooey and truffle-like.

Serves 12

250g unsalted butter

300g dark chocolate (minimum 70% cocoa solids)

365g light brown muscovado sugar

135g ground hazelnuts (blend whole hazelnuts for about 2 minutes in a food processor)

85g cocoa powder, plus extra for dusting

6 large eggs

1 vanilla pod, split and seeds scraped out (or 1 teaspoon vanilla extract)

1½ teaspoons sea salt flakes

Preheat the oven to 180°C/160°C fan/350°F/Gas mark 4. Grease and line a 23cm round baking tin.

Melt the butter and chocolate in a bowl set over a pan of simmering water. Whisk to combine, then add the sugar and sift in the ground hazelnuts and cocoa powder.

Add the eggs, vanilla seeds and salt, giving it a good stir to mix. Pour the batter into the baking tin and bake for 30 minutes. After this time the cake should have risen but will still have a slight wobble in the centre.

Remove from the oven and leave to cool slightly before serving it with Salted Caramel Chocolate Sauce (see page 215) and vanilla ice cream. It will stay gooey for several days wrapped in cling film.

Steamed Chocolate Pudding

Do you remember school dinners? Was there anything more reassuring than chocolate sponge and custard?

Serves 6

75g **unsalted butter**

70g **cocoa powder**

190g **dark brown muscovado sugar**

225g **full-fat milk**

75g **self-raising flour, sifted**

25g **plain flour, sifted**

75g **brioche crumbs or breadcrumbs**

¼ **teaspoon sea salt flakes**

2 **egg yolks**

Melt the butter in a small saucepan over a medium heat until brown. Remove from the heat and leave to cool.

Sift the cocoa powder and sugar into a bowl to combine, then slowly whisk in the milk until you are left with a thick chocolate paste. Add the browned butter and whisk again. Stir in the flours, brioche crumbs or breadcrumbs, salt and finally, the egg yolks. The mixture should be thick and shiny.

Pour into a greased and floured 500ml pudding basin and prepare the pudding for steaming (see page 13). Place a large saucepan over a high heat, put the pudding inside and fill the pan halfway to two-thirds up the pudding basin with freshly boiled water. Quickly put a lid on and leave to boil for 1 hour and 15 minutes. Keep the water topped up with more boiling water if necessary. The pudding is done when it has risen fully and the sponge is springy to touch.

To serve, remove the pudding from the saucepan. Take off the string and foil and run a small knife around the edge of the pudding to loosen. Place a warmed plate on top and invert the pudding onto the plate. Serve immediately with warm vanilla or chocolate custard, or both (why not?).

Tip: If you're feeling brave, remove the pudding from the saucepan after 45 minutes to 1 hour. At this point the pudding will still have a gooey centre. Serve immediately with some extra custard just in case it's not as gooey as you'd like.

Baked Chocolate Tart

Before I started The Pudding Stop, my wife Jennifer was the baker of the house. And, this was her speciality. I teased her for a long time that it was more like a cake – but we've since adapted it together, and now it's perfect.

Serves 8-10

1 batch Shortcrust Pastry (see page 20)

Flour, for dusting

400g dark chocolate (minimum 70% cocoa solids)

200g unsalted butter

2 tablespoon cocoa powder

150g light brown muscovado sugar

A pinch of sea salt

4 large eggs, plus 2 large egg yolks

Preheat the oven to 180°C/160°C fan/350°F/Gas mark 4.

Roll out the pastry on a lightly floured work surface to about 3mm thick. Use it to line a greased 23cm loose-bottomed tart tin, prick the pastry all over with a fork and chill for 30 minutes.

Once chilled, cover the pastry with foil, fill with baking beans and bake blind for about 15 minutes, until golden brown around the edges.

Remove the foil and baking beans and return the pastry case to the oven for 1–2 minutes, until it is a pale brown colour all over. Remove from the oven and leave to cool. Increase the oven temperature to 200°C/180°C fan/400°F/Gas mark 6.

For the filling, melt the chocolate and butter in a bowl set over a pan of simmering water. Once melted, whisk in in the cocoa, sugar and salt. Leave to cool slightly, then whisk in the eggs and yolks.

Pour the filling into the pastry case and bake for 10–15 minutes. It is ready when the mixture has risen slightly and a wobble remains in the centre. Remove from the oven and serve immediately – the centre may still be a little runny, but it is cooked, and what's better than molten chocolate? Alternatively, leave to cool and place it in the fridge to firm up – the perfect picnic accompaniment. Serve with crème fraîche.

Tip: It is essential that you whisk in, rather than beat, the eggs to ensure they are fully combined with the rest of the mixture.

Salted Caramel & Peanut Butter Chocolate Brownies

These brownies are exquisite – what a pity they aren't illegal.

Makes 15

550g dark chocolate (minimum 70% cocoa solids)

275g unsalted butter

7 large eggs

675g light brown soft sugar

1½ teaspoons vanilla extract

325g plain flour

5½ tablespoons cocoa powder

½ teaspoon flaked sea salt

6–8 tablespoons chunky peanut butter (at room temperature)

For the salted caramel filling

525g caster sugar

450ml double cream

30g unsalted butter

2 teaspoons sea salt flakes, or to taste

For the roasted peanuts

50g unsalted peanuts

Sea salt flakes

First, make the filling. Place the sugar and 4 tablespoons water in a large saucepan over a high heat and melt until the sugar has caramelised and turned the colour of an old penny. Remove from the heat and very carefully pour in the cream – the mixture will bubble and erupt ferociously at first, but will settle.

Place the pan back on the heat and let the caramel melt into the cream. Turn the heat up again to a rolling simmer, and keep whisking until you have a smooth dark caramel. Whisk in the butter and salt. Pour into a bowl or plastic container and leave to chill in the fridge until fully cold.

Next, roast the peanuts. Preheat the oven to 180°C/160°C fan/350°F/Gas mark 4. Spread the peanuts out on a baking tray in an even layer. Sprinkle with sea salt and bake for 15 minutes. Set aside to cool, but leave the oven on while you make the brownie batter.

For the brownies, melt the chocolate and butter in a bowl set over a pan of simmering water, then set aside to cool. Whisk the eggs, sugar and vanilla in another bowl until fully combined. Add the egg mixture to the chocolate mixture. Sift the flour and cocoa into another bowl, then fold into the brownie mixture.

Split the mixture in half and pour one half into a 35 x 25 x 5cm baking tin that has been lined with baking parchment, then put it in the fridge to chill. Cover the other half and leave in a warm place to ensure it doesn't dry out.

Once the first batch is fully chilled, after about 30 minutes, remove it from the fridge and spread over the salted caramel filling and sprinkle over the roasted peanuts. Cover with the second half of brownie mixture and use a palette knife to smooth and flatten the mixture, being very careful not to disturb the caramel underneath.

Dot 6–8 tablespoons of chunky peanut butter intermittently on top and swirl through gently. Bake for 30–35 minutes, until mounds appear and a slight wobble remains. Leave to cool completely until set, before cutting into squares. You can place in the fridge to speed this process up if needed.

Chocolate Madeleines

Adding chocolate chips to these delicious madeleines means there's a little melting chocolate moment in almost every bite. Madeleines do keep well for a few days in an airtight container, and a day-old madeleine dunks into tea very nicely.

Makes about 24

135g unsalted butter, plus extra, melted, for brushing

2 tablespoons golden syrup

3 large eggs

125g light brown soft sugar

100g self-raising flour, sifted, plus extra for dusting

30g cocoa powder, sifted

A handful of chocolate chips

Place a saucepan over a medium heat and melt the butter with the golden syrup until it turns golden brown. Set aside to cool.

Whisk the eggs and sugar in a stand mixer until the mixture's volume has tripled. To check if the mixture is ready, lift the whisk out of the mixture; a trail should remain on the surface for a couple of seconds. Fold in the flour and cocoa powder, then the melted butter mixture until well incorporated and glossy. Cover and leave in the fridge until ready to use. Ideally the mixture needs a few hours to settle.

Preheat the oven to 200°C/180°C fan/400°F/Gas mark 6. Brush a madeleine tray with melted butter and dust with flour, then invert and bang the tray on the work surface to remove any excess flour.

Divide the batter equally between each madeleine shell, then dot about six chocolate chips into each one. Be careful to not over-fill – the mixture will rise during baking, and therefore two-thirds full will be enough.

Bake for 8–10 minutes, or until a beautiful golden brown peak has formed. Remove from the oven and leave to rest for a few moments. Carefully remove each one from the madeleine tray and place on a plate with a side bowl of chocolate sauce or simply a nice pot of tea.

Tip: The madeleine batter will keep well in the fridge for 3–4 days allowing you to bake half a dozen a day as a little tea-time treat.

Rocky Road

The perfect antidote to a life led along a rocky road. I like to eat them cut into little squares with a warm coffee, alternating between a sip of coffee and a bite of rocky road: a very relaxing five minutes well spent in what is otherwise a hectic day. This Rocky Road can also be used to make my Rocky Road Sundae (see page 152).

Makes 15 squares

250g unsalted butter

600g dark chocolate (minimum 60% cocoa solids)

90g maple or golden syrup

600g chocolate digestives, bashed into chunky pieces

200g raisins or prunes

200g white mini marshmallows

100g chopped pecans

A large pinch of sea salt

1 teaspoon vanilla extract

For the chocolate topping

45g unsalted butter

150g dark chocolate (minimum 60% cocoa solids)

25g maple or golden syrup

Melt the butter with the chocolate and syrup in a saucepan over a medium to low heat, stirring continuously to prevent the chocolate from sticking and burning. Add all the remaining ingredients, and stir until well combined.

Pour into a 35 x 25 x 5cm baking tray lined with baking parchment.

To make the topping, melt the butter, chocolate and maple syrup in a saucepan over a low heat, until melted and glossy. Pour over the rocky road to create a shiny, chocolatey top. Chill in the fridge for a few hours until set, or overnight.

Rocky road stores for several days in an airtight container in the fridge or a cool place.

Chocolate Mousse

My mum has this silly little cookbook in her kitchen, and in it are silly little cartoon chefs holding giant wooden spoons giving important instructions throughout recipes. It's over 30 years old, and completely knackered, but their pointers must be helpful. She always makes a chocolate mousse a bit like this one and it never fails to keep the family happy.

Makes 4

150g dark chocolate (minimum 70% cocoa solids)

A pinch of sea salt

4 large eggs, separated

200g milk or dark chocolate, to garnish

Melt the dark chocolate in a bowl set over a saucepan of simmering water until melted and glossy.

Add a pinch of salt to the egg whites and whisk them until soft peaks form, but do not over-whisk.

Beat the egg yolks into the chocolate. Use a large metal spoon to add a spoonful of whites to the chocolate mixture, and very carefully fold it in, followed by the rest of the whites.

Divide between four ramekins and place in the fridge for 2–3 hours to set.

Use a sharp kitchen knife to scrape shards of chocolate (or you could use a grater) over each mousse, and serve immediately.

Festive

Mincemeat Tart

Christmas Pudding

Plum Pudding

Mince Pie Ice Cream

Mulled Wine Jelly Shots

Eggnog Pudding

Steamed Marzipan Pudding

Chocolate Log

Rose's Madeleines

Ralph's Festive Rocky Road

Figgy Frangipane

Festive times are there to celebrate in a merry, joyful and exuberant way – so surround yourself with good people and good food. In Britain, being festive is synonymous with Christmas and Easter. This chapter's focus is Christmas – the time of the year when most people will have the chance to be together with friends and family, and when you will want to make the most effort for those visiting or being visited. For many, Christmas is chocolate, chocolate, and more chocolate yet there's so much more on offer.

Towards the end of summer it will be time to start thinking about Christmas. Well, your Christmas pudding, anyway. We always make ours in August when the shop is quieter and the steam oven is used less frequently. Allowing your Christmas puddings to mature over six months, and feeding them well with brandy, will cause a real stir come Christmas Day. Homemade mincemeat is a must, and will transform the opinion of any mince pie-doubters. For those looking for something a little lighter around Christmastime, my Eggnog Pudding – like a whopping wobbly panna cotta – will be sure to wow your visitors, especially if you greet them at the door with cheeky little shots of my Mulled Wine Jelly.

Mincemeat Tart

This is like a massive mince pie, but with mascarpone and clementines to take the mincemeat to another level. Baking the mincemeat before it goes in the tart will help to intensify the flavour.

Serves 10

500g Homemade Mincemeat (see page 222)

1 batch of Shortcrust Pastry (see page 20)

Flour, for dusting

50g icing sugar

1 egg yolk

Grated zest and juice of 2 clementines

300g mascarpone

A handful of flaked almonds

A handful of demerara sugar

Preheat the oven to 200°C/180°C fan/400°F/Gas mark 6. Spread the mincemeat out on a lightly greased baking tray and bake for 15–20 minutes, or until it is caramelised and sticky. Remove from the oven and spoon into a dish to cool. Reduce the oven temperature to 180°C/160°C fan/350°F/Gas mark 4.

Roll out the pastry on a lightly floured work surface to about 3mm thick. Use it to line a greased 23cm loose-bottomed tart tin, prick the base all over with a fork, then put it in the fridge to chill for 30 minutes. Line the pastry case with foil, fill with baking beans and bake for about 15 minutes, until golden brown around the edges. Remove the foil and baking beans and return the pastry case to the oven until it is a golden brown colour all over. Remove from the oven and leave to cool. Keep the oven on at the same temperature.

Spread the baked mincemeat over the base of the tart. Whisk the icing sugar, egg yolk and clementine zest and juice into the mascarpone and spread this on top of the mincemeat. Sprinkle over the almonds and demerara sugar and bake for 25–30 minutes, until the mascarpone is golden brown. Remove from the oven and leave to cool slightly, before cutting into slices and serving with brandy butter.

Christmas Pudding

Makes three 900g puddings (each serving 8–10)

225g fresh beef suet or dried vegetarian suet

275g breadcrumbs (sourdough or brioche)

225g self-raising flour

450g dark brown muscovado sugar

350g sultanas

350g Muscatel raisins

450g currants

500g candied mixed fruit peel

450g glacé cherries

225g flaked almonds

Grated zest and juice of 1 lemon

Grated zest and juice of 1 orange

1 whole nutmeg, finely grated

1½ teaspoons ground cloves

1 tablespoon ground cinnamon

6 large eggs

425ml stout

6 tablespoons brandy, plus 1 tablespoon per pudding per month to feed

Always make at least three Christmas puddings. One for Christmas Day, one to remind yourself how good it was a few days later and one to keep for the following year or to give as a present. My grandmother always insisted that we fry leftover Christmas pudding in brandy butter. This is her recipe. In the early days of the business and before I could afford to buy a fancy steam oven, I would steam hundreds of puddings on the stove at home day and night. To help, my grandmother would insist on steaming half of them, asking me to drop them off at her house after my farmers' market nearby. All this during the peak of a warm British summer in London – a pudding made in the summer, given a little drink of brandy each month and time to settle, is a far better pudding.

Place all the ingredients, except for the flour and eggs, into a large bowl and stir to combine. Cover and leave for 1–2 days for the ingredients to acquaint themselves with each other.

A day or so later add the flour and the eggs. Give the mixture another stir and divide evenly between three 1-litre pudding basins. Cover with baking parchment and then foil. Secure with string under the rim and make a loop over the top to form a handle.

Steam for 9 hours in a large pan of boiling water, making sure the water does not boil away.

When cooked, leave to cool, then add 1 tablespoon brandy to each pudding and replace the baking parchment and foil. Store in a cool-dry place repeating the 1 tablespoon brandy per pudding every month until Christmas.

When ready to eat, steam each pudding for at least a further 3 hours before serving.

Tip: It is essential that you steam the pudding for 9 hours at first, and a further 3 hours on the day of eating to create a really light and tasty pudding. If you don't, my granny will come knocking.

Plum Pudding

Plum pudding was the original Christmas pudding in pre-Victorian times, when raisins were known as plums, and it is a fruitier version of the Christmas pud of today. Its association with Christmas appears to come from King George I (the Pudding King) requesting plum pudding for his first Christmas in England. Soon after, the Christmas pudding became the most treasured part of the nation's festive traditions.

In modern times, the plum pudding has lost favour with younger generations, but stir-up Sunday – a tradition urging the whole family to make the pudding together on the last Sunday before Advent – has helped to keep this pud on Christmas tables. I urge you to no longer buy a supermarket pudding – try this or my aforementioned grandmother's Christmas Pudding recipe (see page 188).

Makes three 900g puddings (each serving 8–10)

225g fresh beef suet or dried vegetarian suet

275g breadcrumbs (sourdough or brioche)

225g self-raising flour

450g dark brown muscovado sugar

350g figs, stalks removed, cut into eighths

350g Victoria plums, stoned and cut into quarters

450g dried pitted prunes, cut in half

500g Bramley apples, peeled, cored and diced

450g fresh cherries

225g flaked almonds

Grated zest and juice of 1 lemon

Grated zest and juice of 1 orange

1 whole nutmeg, finely grated

1½ teaspoons ground gloves

1 tablespoon ground cinnamon

6 large eggs

425ml stout

6 tablespoons brandy, plus 1 tablespoon per pudding per month, to feed

Place all the ingredients, except for the flour and eggs, into a large bowl and stir to combine. Cover and leave for 1–2 days for the ingredients to acquaint themselves with each other.

A day or so later add the flour and eggs. Give the mixture another stir and divide evenly between three 1-litre pudding basins. Cover with baking parchment and then foil. Secure with string under the rim and make a loop over the top to form a handle.

Steam for 9 hours in a large pan of boiling water, making sure the water does not boil away.

When cooked, leave to cool, then add 1 tablespoon brandy to each pudding and replace the baking parchment and foil. Store in a cool, dry place repeating the 1 tablespoon brandy per pudding every month until Christmas.

When ready to eat, steam each pudding for at least a further 3 hours before serving.

Mince Pie Ice Cream

This recipe is for those of you who either cannot eat pastry or cannot be bothered to make it and roll it out into mince pies. This way you get all the pleasure that a mince pie gives, with none of the effort.

Makes 1 litre

500g vanilla ice cream

500g Homemade Mincemeat (see page 224)

Take the ice cream out of the freezer to soften slightly. Empty it into a food processor or blender and beat in the mincemeat.

Pour back into a larger container and freeze. After several hours or overnight it will be ready to eat. Try serving with a tablespoon of flaming brandy poured over.

Mulled Wine Jelly Shots

This jelly is counterintuitive, as it eliminates the warm glow that mulled wine brings on a cold December night. However, this jelly demonstrates the genius flavour combinations that go into a decent mulled wine – to be celebrated and enjoyed warm or cold. Do not be tempted to buy a 'bottle of mulled wine' or to use cheap plonk; it will only bring disappointment with your jelly.

Makes 8

250g caster sugar

2 bay leaves

1 cinnamon stick

6 whole cloves

6 allspice

1 star anise

1 orange, peel carefully removed and juice squeezed out

1 bottle of tasty red wine (Malbec works well)

15g bronze leaf gelatine

About 1 teaspoon gold leaf, to decorate (optional)

Put all the ingredients, except for the wine and gelatine, in a saucepan over a medium heat. Pour over just enough wine to cover the sugar. Bring to the boil and keep on a rolling boil until you have thick syrup. This will ensure that the spices infuse well into the wine.

Turn down the heat and add the remaining wine. Cook on a low simmer for a further 10 minutes. Remove from the heat and set aside.

Meanwhile, soak the gelatine in a bowl of cold water until soft and tactile. Drain and squeeze the gelatine to remove any excess water.

Once the mulled wine reaches blood temperature, strain it through a sieve and whisk in the soaked gelatine. Pass through the sieve again and into individual shot glasses. Chill for several hours or overnight and when set, decorate with gold leaf, if you are using it.

Greet your guests at the door with a shot of mulled wine and a freshly baked Rose's Madeleine (see page 202).

Eggnog Pudding

Eggnog is a British invention. Yes, really. It is thought to have evolved from the ubiquitous posset of the eighteenth century – remember that warmed beverage served in spouted cups or glasses whereby the froth and liquid could be drunk separately? Well I suppose adding egg was just a natural progression to add richness and texture. The word 'nog' came from a drinking cup – the noggin – carved from an English tree, which in turn was named for holding the much-loved strong ale brewed in Norfolk at the time, called nog. This means that you must include the booze to make true (egg)nog!

Makes 10

400ml full-fat milk

400ml double cream

1 vanilla pod, split and seeds scraped out

1 cinnamon stick

1 teaspoon freshly grated nutmeg, plus extra to grate on top

30g bronze leaf gelatine

200g caster sugar

600ml buttermilk

250g dark rum or Bourbon

Heat the milk, cream, split vanilla pod and seeds, cinnamon and nutmeg in a saucepan and bring to the boil. Take off the heat and set aside for all of those lovely spices to infuse into the milk and cream.

Soak the gelatine in a bowl of cold water for about 5 minutes, or until soft, then drain and squeeze out any excess water. Leave in the bowl until ready.

When the milk has cooled slightly to blood temperature, whisk in the sugar, followed by the soaked gelatine. Be careful at this point – if the mixture is too hot the composition of the gelatine will change and it will not set the liquid, too cold and it won't dissolve.

When the mixture reaches room temperature, whisk in the buttermilk, then the rum or bourbon. Pour the eggnog mixture into ten glasses or dariole molds and place in the fridge to set for a few hours, or preferably overnight.

The following day, submerge each of the pudding, in a bowl of warm water and use a finger to encourage the set eggnog to come away from the sides of the mould slightly. Place an inverted plate on top and, holding both plate and mould, give a little shake – you should feel or even hear the pudding release itself from within. Carefully remove the mould.

Liberally grate (ideally with a microplane grater) nutmeg over the top of the puddings. Serve with shortbread and some Pedro-Pimped Prunes (see page 226). The little puddings will last a good few days in the fridge.

Steamed Marzipan Pudding

This pudding has all the flavours of a Bakewell tart in a steamed sponge – jam, almonds, custard and a hidden layer of molten marzipane in the centre of each pudding is such a dream combination. It is important that the frangipane isn't too runny in order for the marzipan to stay in the middle of the pudding throughout. This is also lovely served at Easter.

Makes 6 puddings

65g unsalted butter

165g caster sugar

A pinch of salt

1 teaspoon baking powder

250g ground almonds

3 large eggs, beaten

300g raspberry jam (50g per pudding)

300g marzipan (50g per pudding)

Cream the butter and sugar in a stand mixer until pale and fluffy.

Mix the salt and baking powder into the ground almonds and toss a handful into the mixer.

With the mixer running slowly, add the eggs, a little at a time, alternating with further handfuls of the almond mixture. Continue to mix until all is incorporated and you have a thick and glossy frangipane.

Spoon 50g of the raspberry jam into the bottom of each pudding basin, followed by some frangipane, filling the basin just under halfway up.

Roll 50g of marzipan into a disc no wider than the diameter of the pudding basin. Submerge it in the centre of the pudding, followed by more frangipane until no more than two-thirds up the pudding basin. Repeat for each pudding.

Place the puddings in a large saucepan, and secure their lids, or use baking parchment and foil with a folded pleat (see page 13 for further instructions); secure with string and make a string handle to easily lift the puddings from the pan. Pour boiling water into the pan no more than two-thirds of the way up each pudding. Steam for 40–60 minutes, or until the puddings are nicely risen.

Carefully remove the puddings from the saucepan, invert each one into a warmed bowl.

Chocolate Log

Serves 10–12

4 eggs

100g soft light brown sugar

A large pinch of sea salt

60g self-raising flour, sifted

40g cocoa powder, sifted

1 teaspoon baking powder

A handful of caster sugar

For the filling

A splash of brandy or dark rum

½ batch of Chocolate Custard (see page 217)

A liberal handful of dried cranberries

A liberal handful of chopped cooked chestnuts

A liberal handful of chopped pitted prunes

Grated zest of 1 clementine

For the topping

25g unsalted butter

150g milk chocolate

50g golden syrup

A pinch of sea salt

150ml double cream

Gold edible lustre dust (optional)

My mother and her five siblings were sent to elocution classes when they were younger, to ensure they spoke the Queen's English. Unsurprisingly it has stuck, and, it often manifests itself at funny moments. Such as when my mother bragged to friends one day that she had made 'the most wonderful chocolate rooo-laard' (or chocolate log to you and me). She was, and continues to be, teased for her poshness. How now brown cow.

Preheat the oven to 180°C/160°C fan/350°F/Gas mark 4. Line a 20 x 30cm baking tray with baking parchment.

Whisk the eggs and sugar in a stand mixer on high for about 5 minutes, or until they have tripled in volume and the mixture is light and leaves a trail when you remove the whisk from the bowl.

Meanwhile, combine the salt, flour, cocoa powder and baking powder in a large bowl. Once the egg mixture is ready, gently fold in the dry ingredients a little at a time, conserving as much air within the batter as possible. It is really worth taking care at this point, as extra care will equate to an extra-special, extra-light sponge.

Spread the sponge batter into the baking tray and bake for 8–10 minutes or until the sponge freely comes away from the sides of the tray.

Once baked, pour half an eggcup of cold water onto the tray beneath the parchment, taking special care not to saturate the sponge. This will help release the sponge from the parchment.

Liberally sprinkle a handful of caster sugar over the sponge, and place a fresh piece of baking parchment and a new cold baking tray or chopping board on top. Carefully invert so that the hot baking tray is on top, and remove the tray and the parchment.

Starting from the long end closest to you, roll up the sponge very tightly until you have formed a Swiss roll. Wedge an object either side of the cake to prevent it from unravelling, and leave until completely cool.

To assemble the log, unroll the sponge and splash a little brandy or rum evenly over the surface. Cover the sponge with a thick layer of Chocolate Custard, followed by all the chopped dried fruit and nuts. Grate over some clementine zest. Roll up the sponge again, taking even more care to roll carefully, and pushing any custard and filling back in that escapes.

For the final topping, melt the butter, chocolate, syrup, salt and cream in a saucepan over a low heat until molten, and whisk until smooth and glossy. Set aside to cool and solidify slightly.

Place the log on a long serving plate and pour over the chocolate topping, trying to cover all parts of the sponge. Once set, dust with gold lustre, if using. It's best eaten the same day – or if wrapped in cling film and placed in the fridge it will still be pretty good the next day.

Rose's Madeleines

These aren't a typical festive treat but they hold sentimental value so I had to include them. My daughter's name is Rose Madeleine and she was born just after the Christmas festivities usually start to slow down, however, we always make sure we continue to be merry until after her birthday. Rosewater is an ingredient that has been added to English trifles, cheesecakes and jellies for centuries. It is as it sounds – a concoction of rose petals steeped in water. It adds a wonderful perfume to food, but must be used cautiously.

Makes about 24

150g butter, melted, plus extra for brushing

2 tablespoons golden syrup

3 large eggs

125g caster sugar

1 teaspoon rosewater

150g self-raising flour, sifted, plus extra for dusting

Put a saucepan over a medium heat and melt the butter with the golden syrup until it turns golden brown. Set aside to cool.

Whisk the eggs, sugar and rosewater in a stand mixer until the mixture's volume has tripled. To check if the mixture is ready, lift the whisk out of the mixture; a trail should remain on the surface for a couple of seconds.

Fold in the flour, then the melted butter mixture and mix until well incorporated and glossy. Cover and leave in the fridge until ready to use. Ideally the mixture needs a few hours to settle.

Preheat the oven to 200°C/180°C fan/400°F/Gas mark 6. Brush a madeleine tray with melted butter and dust with flour – turn it over and bang down the tray to remove any excess flour. Spread the mixture between each hole, being careful to not over-fill. The mixture will rise during baking, and therefore two-thirds full will be enough.

Bake for 8–10 minutes, or until a beautiful golden brown peak is formed. Remove from the oven and leave to rest for a few moments. Carefully remove from the madeleine tray and place on a plate.

Tip: Baked madeleines will keep very well in a sealed tin for up to a week. The older they become the better they are at soaking up tea. Alternatively, the madeleine batter will keep very well in the fridge for 3–4 days, allowing you to bake half a dozen a day as a little tea-time treat.

Ralph's Festive Rocky Road

Ralph has been a customer of The Pudding Stop since the beginning and his enthusiasm and love for traditional puddings is astounding. His favourites include summer pudding and spotted dick or any sort of steamed pudding. I was therefore surprised when he offered up this recipe to me – a far more modern and sweet confection than I had come to expect from him. However, on reading the recipe I was reminded that Ralph is a man who has such a love of pudding and an appreciation of when things are done properly, that this may be the best rocky road you will ever eat.

Makes 20 pieces

600g large raisins (the drier the better)

200g dried cranberries

300ml brandy

3 large tablespoons cocoa powder

125g unsalted butter

200g shortbread biscuits, broken in a bag with a rolling pin

100g pecans, broken in a bag with a rolling pin

750g milk chocolate

250g dark chocolate

Gold edible Lustre dust (optional)

Soak the dried fruit in the brandy for 1 week, until virtually all the brandy has been absorbed.

Line a 30 x 40cm baking tin with baking parchment and set aside.

Put the cocoa in a bowl with any dribbles of brandy left from the soaked fruit and mix to a paste (it should be only just emulsified).

Put the chocolate paste in a saucepan over a gentle heat and add the butter. Mix in until the butter has melted and the cocoa is like thick hot chocolate.

Put the broken biscuits and pecans in a bowl, add the soaked fruit and mix together. Add the cocoa mixture and stir through so that everything is lightly coated in the liquid cocoa.

Melt the two chocolates in a bowl set over a pan of simmering water. Add the melted chocolate to the biscuit mixture and stir well together.

Spoon the mixture into the prepared tin and press into an even layer. Transfer to the fridge to set for 2–3 hours or overnight. Cut into squares once fully set and decorate with edible gold Lustre, if using.

Figgy Frangipane

Oh, bring us a figgy pudding;

Oh, bring us a figgy pudding;

Oh, bring us a figgy pudding and a cup of good cheer

We won't go until we get some;

We won't go until we get some;

We won't go until we get some, so bring some out here

Make sure you find really nice ripe and soft figs. The figs will caramelise in the oven with the honey and almonds, sinking into the duvet of almond frangipane while the pastry puffs up like a springy mattress. You may need a lie down afterwards.

Serves 8

25g unsalted butter

75g caster sugar

A pinch of sea salt

125g ground almonds

1 teaspoon almond extract

2 large eggs, beaten, plus 1 egg yolk

250g Quick Puff Pastry (see page 23)

Flour, for dusting

8 ripe figs, cut into halves

A drizzle of runny honey

2 tablespoons flaked almonds

Preheat the oven to 180°C/160°C fan/350°F/Gas mark 4.

Cream the butter and sugar in a stand mixer until pale and fluffy. In another bowl, add the salt to the almonds and toss in a handful into the mixer. Mix the almond extract into the beaten eggs.

With the mixer running slowly, add the eggs, a little at a time, alternating with further handfuls of almonds. Continue to mix until all is incorporated and you have a thick and glossy frangipane. If it looks too wet, add a little more ground almond.

Roll out the pastry on a floured work surface to 5mm thick, rolling it to fit snugly within a 23cm baking tray. Carefully transfer the rolled-out pastry onto a baking tray lined with greaseproof paper. Spread the frangipane over the surface of the pastry, leaving a small perimeter around the edge. Brush the perimeter with the egg yolk.

Lay the fig halves on top in any pattern you wish and cover with a drizzle of honey and the flaked almonds.

Bake for 20–25 minutes, or until the figs are soft and the pastry is golden brown. Serve immediately with vanilla ice cream.

On the Side

Toffee Sauce

Butterscotch Sauce

Salted Caramel Sauce

Salted Caramel Chocolate Sauce

Custard

Caramel Custard

Chocolate Custard

Almond Milk

Brown Sugar Almond Custard

Homemade Mincemeat

Brandy Butter

Vanilla Cream

Simple Blueberry Jam

Pedro-Pimped Prunes

Shortbread

Lemon Curd

This is arguably the most important chapter; it is this chapter that makes a pudding a pudding. What would sticky toffee pudding be without toffee sauce, or crumble with no custard?

All of these magical bits on the side can elevate a simple cake into a pleasurable and potent pudding – as with my Plum & Stem Ginger Pudding and Butterscotch Sauce. Furthermore, these chocolate, butterscotch and toffee sauces link individual constituent parts within a recipe, as with the Banoffee Bocker Glory (see page 146) or Rocky Road Sundae (see page 152). Accompaniments like Vanilla Cream (see page 223), Shortbread (see page 227) or Pedro-Pimped Prunes (see page 226) can add appeal and texture to an otherwise ordinary pud.

There is perhaps nothing simpler, yet more pleasing, than a scoop of vanilla ice cream with chocolate sauce. It can make even the most Falstaffian of gents giddy at the knees. And after all, if nothing else, what's wrong with just drinking custard straight from the jug?

Toffee Sauce

This thick, rich, dark brown sauce has been poured over sticky toffee pudding since its inception. I encourage you to pour some of this sauce on your toffee pudding as soon as it's removed from the oven. It's the same colour as the pudding and seeps all the way through, creating an incredibly moist and unctuous dessert.

Makes about 500ml

130g soft dark brown sugar

70g black treacle

100g unsalted butter

150ml double cream

A pinch of sea salt

Put all the ingredients together in a saucepan over a medium heat. Melt and whisk to combine while you bring the mixture to the boil. Take the pan off the heat and set aside. Reheat when needed if necessary. The sauce will keep in the fridge for several days (in a sterilised jar it could last 1–2 weeks).

Tip: Warm the tin of treacle on the stove to make it easier to pour; the flow of treacle will be faster and thinner.

Butterscotch Sauce

Liquid Werther's Originals. In a good way.

Makes 500ml

125g caster sugar
300ml double cream
65g unsalted butter

Put the sugar and 2 tablespoons of cold water in a saucepan over a medium heat. Cook so that the sugar melts and turns into a caramel. Keep cooking until the caramel is a rich, dark colour similar to an old penny.

Take the pan off the heat and pour in the double cream – it will spit and bubble but will then settle down. Put the pan back over a medium heat and whisk to allow the caramel to melt into the cream.

Keep cooking over a high heat until thick and golden, before finally whisking in the butter. It is now ready to add to a pudding, and keeps very well in the fridge for up to a week.

Salted Caramel Sauce

Salted caramel. Just a fad? Not any more.

Makes 1 litre

525g caster sugar

450ml double cream

30g unsalted butter

2 teaspoons flaked sea salt

Put the sugar and 4 tablespoons of cold water in a saucepan over a medium heat. Cook, swirling the pan, until the sugar melts and turns into a caramel – swirl do not be tempted to stir. Keep cooking until the caramel is a rich, dark colour similar to an old penny.

Take the pan off the heat and pour in the double cream – it will spit and bubble but will then settle down.

Put the pan back over a medium heat and whisk to allow the caramel to melt into the cream.

Keep cooking over a high heat until thick and golden before finally whisking in the butter and salt. It is now ready to add to a pudding, or to be cooled for the Salted Caramel & Peanut Butter Chocolate Brownies (see page 174). The sauce will keep in the fridge for 2–3 days.

Salted Caramel Chocolate Sauce

At The Pudding Stop, we pour a little of this sauce over our Flourless Chocolate Cake (see page 168), served slightly warmed with a scoop of vanilla or milk ice cream. It is also excellent for dunking freshly baked Chocolate Madeleines (see page 176) or simply poured over ice cream.

Makes 1 litre

300g unsalted butter

300g soft brown light sugar

10g flaked sea salt

300ml double cream

100g dark chocolate (minimum 70% cocoa solids)

Melt the butter and sugar in a saucepan over a medium heat, and whisk together. Add the salt, cream and chocolate and turn the heat up. Whisk continuously, until you have a thick glossy sauce. The sauce will keep in the fridge for several days (in a sterilised jar it could last 1–2 weeks).

Custard

'Let this a warning be to you that go to Islington, custard will kill, experience shows, as quick as any gun. Beware you that on holydays abroad do feast your wives, for you that feed on custard go in danger of your lives.' Anonymous

Makes about 1 litre

625ml double cream

1 vanilla pod, split and seeds scraped out

7 large egg yolks

75g caster sugar

Put the cream and vanilla in a saucepan over a medium heat and bring to the boil. Take the pan off the heat and set aside for the vanilla to infuse while you whisk the eggs and sugar.

Whisk the egg yolks and sugar together in a bowl until just mixed, then pour the hot cream over the eggs, whisking all the time.

Pass the mixture through a sieve into a clean saucepan and place back over a medium heat. Cook slowly, still whisking, until the custard is thick and coats the back of a spoon.

The custard will keep for 2 days in the fridge and can be reheated in a saucepan. Make lots and you'll have it when most needed.

Caramel Custard

To get this custard right you need to be prepared to go to the precipice between burning the caramel and arriving at a dark nutty caramel the colour of an old penny. This custard is brilliant with puddings such as crumble and spotted dick, or can add another level of flavour to your trifle.

Makes about 1 litre

600g caster sugar

625ml double cream

1 vanilla pod, split and seeds scraped out

7 large egg yolks

Put 525g of the sugar and 4 tablespoons of cold water in a saucepan over a medium heat. Cook so that the sugar melts and turns into a caramel. Keep cooking until the caramel is a rich, dark colour similar to an old penny.

Put the cream and split vanilla pod and seeds in a saucepan over a medium heat and bring to the boil. Set aside for the vanilla to infuse.

Whisk the egg yolks and the remaining 75g sugar in a bowl, then pour the hot cream over the eggs, whisking all the time. Pass the mixture through a sieve into the saucepan of caramel.

Put the caramel and custard pan back over a medium heat and warm slowly so that you can whisk the caramel into the custard. Continue to whisk and cook the custard until it is thick and can coat the back of a spoon. The custard will keep in the fridge for 2 days.

Chocolate Custard

Chocolate custard! You really can't get much better than this.

Makes 700ml

250ml double cream

250ml full-fat milk

6 large egg yolks

70g caster sugar

30g plain flour

100g dark chocolate
(minimum 70%
cocoa solids)

Put the cream and milk in a heavy-based saucepan over a medium heat and bring to the boil.

Whisk the egg yolks and sugar in a bowl, then sift in the flour and whisk together.

Once the milk has boiled, carefully pour it into the bowl, whisking continuously. Return the whole mixture back to the pan and bring back to the boil over a low heat. Keep whisking to ensure the custard is evenly distributed in the pan and is not sticking.

When the custard reaches the boil, keep whisking for 5 minutes until it is very thick.

Strain through a sieve into a bowl and whisk in the chocolate until fully combined and smooth. Pour into a warmed jug and serve immediately. It will keep well in the fridge for 2 days.

Brandy Butter

Toffee Sauce

Vanilla Cream

Butterscotch Sauce

Almond Milk

*Salted Caramel
Chocolate Sauce*

Custard

Almond Milk

You can of course buy your own almond milk, but the process of making it will be as healing for your soul as drinking the aforementioned liquid. You can make a big or small batch – but it does keep very well for a week in the fridge – and I always encourage big batches.

Makes about 500ml

150g of whole almonds to 500ml of water is the ratio to use – so you can make as much as you like

Soak the almonds and water for at least 2 days prior to making the almond milk. The longer you soak,, the creamier the milk.

Strain the almonds, reserving the liquid, and rinse the almonds under a tap of cold water.

Put the almonds and the reserved liquid in a food processor or blender, and blend continuously for up to 5 minutes, until the almonds are as fine as they will go. You may need to stop to scrape down the sides during the process.

Pour the contents of the blender through a muslin cloth set inside a sieve into a bowl. Once the majority of the almond milk has passed through, draw together the ends of the muslin cloth and squeeze out every last morsel of almond milk.

Tip: Looking for dairy-free? Use this almond milk to make my Brown Sugar Almond Custard (see page opposite), which can be served warm with any poached fruits or the dairy-free Bramley Apple Upside Down Pudding (see page 74).

Brown Sugar Almond Custard

Swapping dairy milk for almond milk creates very tasty custard and is a lovely alternative to serve with my dairy-free Bramley Apple Upside Down Pudding (see page 74).

Makes about 1 litre

500ml Almond Milk (see opposite page or shop-bought)

1 vanilla pod, split and seeds scraped out

6 egg yolks

50g dark brown soft sugar

2 tablespoons maple syrup

4 teaspoons cornflour

Put the almond milk and split vanilla pod and seeds in a saucepan and bring to the boil.

In a bowl, whisk the egg yolks, sugar, maple syrup and cornflour until smooth.

Whisk in the hot almond milk, then return the mixture to the pan and set on a medium heat. Continue to whisk until the custard is thick and it coats the back of a spoon.

The custard will keep for 2 days in the fridge and can be reheated in a saucepan.

Homemade Mincemeat

Make the mincemeat 1–2 months ahead of Christmas, as it matures and the flavour improves with time. This recipe will make more than you need for the Mincemeat Tart on page 188 – store the leftover mincemeat in a clean airtight jar and it will keep for 6–12 months if the jar has been sterilised and sealed properly.

Makes about 1kg

110g Muscatel raisins

220g currants

55g sultanas

140g Bramley apples, peeled and chopped

140g dark brown muscovado sugar

85g suet

85g candied mixed fruit peel

85g glacé cherries

Grated zest and juice of 1 lemon

Grated zest and juice of 1 orange

40g flaked almonds

1 teaspoon ground mixed spice

1 teaspoon freshly grated nutmeg

75ml brandy

25ml port

Combine all the ingredients in a bowl, and store in an airtight container or preferably in sterilised Kilner or preserve jars.

Leave for 1–2 months for the flavours to intensify.

Tip: Try to source Muscatel raisins – they are larger and darker than a regular raisins and really add to the quality of mincemeat come Christmas.

Brandy Butter

The simplicity of making your own brandy butter means you need never fear running out – and you can therefore make your guests even happier with bigger dollops to accompany their Christmas Pudding (see page 190) or mince pie.

Makes enough for 12 mince pies

250g unsalted butter

250g caster sugar

60ml boiling water

100ml brandy

Cream the butter and sugar until pale and fluffy. Stir in the boiling water and brandy until smooth and well incorporated. Place in the fridge to firm up a little, then it is ready to use. The brandy butter will keep in the fridge for 2–3 days.

Vanilla Cream

Adding sugar to cream not only sweetens it but also stiffens it and guards against over-whipping. If you use an electric whisk, start on a very slow setting so you have full control; for small batches, I would always encourage whisking by hand. Stop whisking as soon as the cream looks silky and can just about hold itself up.

Serves 4

200ml double cream

120g caster sugar

1 vanilla pod, split and seeds scraped out

Put the cream, sugar and scraped vanilla seeds in a bowl and whisk until it just forms very soft peaks. This is best eaten straightaway. Serve with jelly, Flourless Chocolate Cake (see page 168), chocolate mousse or any tart.

Simple Blueberry Jam

Using seasonal summer fruit to make jam is quick and easy – no special sugar or pectin required. One of my favourites is blueberry, which I've included here.

Makes 500g

500g blueberries

375g granulated sugar

Put the fruit and sugar in a large saucepan or preserving pan over a medium heat. Bring to the boil and simmer for 25 minutes, until soft and sticky and jam-like.

You can test the consistency of your jam by placing a hot dollop on a cold plate that has been in the freezer for a while. Run your finger through the middle of the jam – it is ready when the jam doesn't seep back into the middle. The jam will keep in the fridge for several days (in an unopened sterilised jar it should last for months).

Tip: Different fruits will need varying levels of preparation before making them into jam:

- *Soft fruits like berries and currants can go in whole.*
- *Rhubarb should be cut and trimmed.*
- *Apples and pears should be peeled, cored and chopped.*
- *Plums, damsons, nectarines, peaches, cherries and apricots should be stoned.*

Pedro-Pimped Prunes

These prunes are an ideal European marriage – Pedro Ximenez sherry from Spain and prunes from France – and what a marriage it is. Try and get your hands on some *pruneaux d'Agen*, or prunes named after the French city of Agen, with their stones still in place – they will be considerably more succulent. Every year in Agen there is a prune spitting competition to celebrate these fabulous dried plums – the winner is the one who spits the prune stone the furthest. I have been lucky enough to attend, and left with a T-shirt!

*Fills a
2-litre jar*

*1 x 70cl bottle of Pedro
Ximenez sherry*

*1kg Agen prunes, with
stones in*

Place the prunes in a steralised 2-litre jar and add the sherry. Leave the lid on for at least a week – they will keep quite happily for a month. Eat them with everything.

Shortbread

The refinement of shortbread, making it suitable for the wealthy and reserved for luxurious celebrations, is credited to Mary Queen of Scots. She is thought to have named them petticoat tails – the circular shortbread cut into neat triangles. It was eaten throughout Scotland on Hogmanay, and broken over the head of new brides on the Shetland Islands as they entered their marital home for the first time. It's also a lovely accompaniment to many puddings in this book.

Makes 15–20 fingers

300g unsalted butter

125g caster sugar, plus more to sprinkle

1½ teaspoons sea salt

425g plain flour, plus extra for dusting

Beat the butter in a bowl until soft. Add the sugar and salt and beat together, followed by the flour.

Line a baking tray with baking parchment. Roll the shortbread dough out on a lightly floured work surface to 1cm thick and cut into biscuits – fingers or round – and place on the baking tray. Sprinkle with caster sugar, then place in the fridge for 30 minutes to chill. Preheat the oven to 180°C/160°C fan/350°F/Gas mark 4.

Bake for 15–20 minutes, until pale and lightly golden but not too coloured.

Remove from the oven and sprinkle liberally with more caster sugar. Leave to cool before storing neatly in an airtight container. You now have a stack of delicious shortbread to keep you going for a month.

Lemon Curd (& Bonus Recipes)

Once you have made everything in my book – what, you haven't yet? – you can have a go at my three bonus recipes (a little like when you buy the deluxe version of an album). Make the lemon curd first (try to source Amalfi lemons if you can), and put it in the fridge until properly chilled. Then crack on with the recipes on the opposite page.

Makes about 500ml

200g caster sugar

100g unsalted butter

Grated zest and juice of 4 whole unwaxed lemons

A pinch of salt

½ vanilla pod, split and seeds scraped out

50ml stem ginger syrup

3 large eggs, plus 2 egg yolks

Put all the ingredients, except the eggs and egg yolks, in a heatproof bowl and set the bowl over a saucepan of simmering water. Cook and whisk together until the butter has melted and the ingredients are well combined.

Whisk the eggs and egg yolks in a separate bowl, and add these to the bowl over the simmering water. Whisk continuously for about 10 minutes, until the lemon mixture starts to thicken and can eventually coat the back of a spoon.

Take the pan off the heat and whisk until it is at room temperature to prevent the curd from curdling. The curd can now be kept in sterilised Kilner jars until ready to use, and will keep for several weeks in the fridge.

Curd Tarts (makes 12 small tarts)

Roll out a batch of Shortcrust Pastry (see page 20) and use it to line a 12-hole shallow tart tin. Prick the base of each with a fork and chill for 30 minutes. Place a big dollop of lemon curd in each pastry case – filling no more than two-thirds full – and bake in an oven preheated to 200°C/180°C fan/400°F/Gas mark 6 for 8–10 minutes, until the pastry is crisp and the curd is bubbling. Take the tarts from the oven and leave to cool for a few moments, before carefully turning each tart out onto a wire rack.

Curd and Blackberry Bakewell Tarts (makes 12 individual tarts)

Roll out a batch of Shortcrust Pastry (see page 20) and use it to line a 12-hole muffin tin. Prick the base of each with a fork and chill for 30 minutes. Place a small dollop of lemon curd in each pastry case – just covering the base of the pastry – and return it to the fridge. Meanwhile, make one batch of Bakewell Tart filling (see page 28) and divide it between the 12 tarts. Push three or four whole blackberries into each tart filling and sprinkle flaked almonds on top to finish. Bake in an oven preheated to 180°C/160°C fan/350°F/Gas mark 4 for 20–25 minutes, until the frangipane is golden brown or lemon curd begins to bubble through. Take the tarts from the oven and leave to cool for a few moments before carefully turning each tart out onto a wire rack. They're great eaten warm, but be cautious of the molten middle.

Curd on Poor Knights of Winsdor

Make the Poor Knights of Winsdor (see page 42). Once cooked, spread each piece liberally with thick lemon curd straight from your Kilner jar and finish with a dollop of crème fraîche and a drizzle of honey.

Index

Acknowledgements

There are so many people to thank for helping me start and consequently grow The Pudding Stop into a thriving shop in my hometown, St Albans. I could never have done it alone nor would I have wanted to.

Raymond Ernest Johns, my grandfather, for inspiring me as a young lad and sharing his passion for baking, cooking and hospitality. And, to the whole Johns family for all the good times.

Arnie Jacobson for convincing me that Earnest Puddings was a terrible name for a pudding business and for suggesting The Pudding Stop could work well. I think it has! Vicky Jacobson for continuing to offer good ideas.

Mandy and Justin James for generously offering the bakery at Redbournbury Watermill when I planned to start the business from my home kitchen – mine being a kitchen not big enough to fulfil my propensity for pudding let alone the whole of St Albans.

Numan Ahmed for coming up with a smashing logo, and Joanna Keiler for introducing us.

Myles and Stuart Hutchins for lending what later became the Pudmobile, and to Jonathan Spencer for suggesting it.

Catherine Morris for championing The Pudding Stop and helping us open our first shop. Together we've turned the most jinxed location in St Albans into a bustling part of the community.

Nic Fine for helping to open the doors at The Pudding Stop and for the continued support and guidance.

Patricia Shepherd for helping to steam all of those Christmas puddings and for showing me what a decent plate of food looked like. Grandpa John would have taken great joy in visiting The Pudding Stop!

The team at The Pudding Stop past and present. Thank you for the hard work and passion you've shown for the business. To those still at Pudstop Towers, here's to the future.

Colin and Dawn Stocker for helping me along the way and for the vast quantities of freshly grown gooseberries. Thanks also for supporting Jenny every time she's had enough!

Alex Markillie, Rob Crowley and Andy Davies for picking up a paintbrush, lifting ovens not designed to be lifted and helping shift stock on rainy market days.

Hannah Shepherd and Raymond Rulach for your unrelenting support and for putting up with incessant pudding chatter around the table.

Mops and Pops, my wonderful parents, for supporting me, teaching me the value of hard work, inspiring me with your insatiable work ethic and for the enthusiasm whenever I pick up the phone.

Jennifer, my beautiful wife, for sticking by through the highs and lows, and for our even more beautiful daughter, Rose.

This book wouldn't have happened without Amanda Harris, my publisher at Orion, who asked me to write a book after hearing me on the BBC Radio 4 Food and Farming Awards. Thank you for phoning and for giving me this once-in-a-lifetime opportunity. *Puddings* would not be such a beauteous creation without the major skills and mad eye for detail possessed by my editor Tamsin English, art director Abi Hartshorne, photographer Andrew Burton and food stylist Lucy O'Reilly. You guys made this book.

Finally, thanks to you for buying this book. I started The Pudding Stop because I wanted to bring good pudding to the people of St Albans. I am delighted that you – perhaps living further away – can now enjoy The Pudding Stop too.

To all of you, my sincere thanks,

Johnny

First published in Great Britain in 2016
by Weidenfeld & Nicolson
Carmelite House, 50 Victoria Embankment
London EC4Y 0DZ
An Hachette UK Company

10 9 8 7 6 5 4 3 2 1

A CIP catalogue record for this book is available from the
British Library.

ISBN: 978 0 297 87052 4

Photography by Andrew Burton
Design and Art Direction by Abi Hartshorne
Edited by Tamsin English
Food styling by Lucy O'Reilly
Copy-edited by Abi Waters
Proofread by Liz Jones
Indexed by Hilary Bird
Photo on page 191 © StockFood/Michael Paul

Printed and bound in China

The Orion Publishing Group's policy is to use papers that
are natural, renewable and recyclable products and made
from wood grown in sustainable forests. The logging and
manufacturing processes are expected to conform to the
environmental regulations of the country of origin.

www.orionbooks.co.uk

For lots more delicious recipes plus articles,
interviews and videos from the best chefs
cooking today visit our blog
bybookorbycook.co.uk

Follow us

 @bybookorcook

Find us

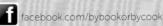 facebook.com/bybookorbycook